EMOTIONAL EDUCATION:

How To Deal With Stress In The Classroom

Before. . . .and After. . . .It Happens

Strategies and Techniques for Educators and Consultants

by

Keith D. Ogburn

Published by
R & E PUBLISHERS
P. O. Box 2008
Saratoga, California 95070

Library of Congress Card Catalog Number
82-60528

I.S.B.N.
0-88247-683-1

To my son,

Cory Todd Ogburn

ACKNOWLEDGMENTS

No person works or develops in isolation. Many people have profoundly influenced the work that I have done. In particular, my gratitude goes to Dr. Don Tiffany who was a constant source of stimulation, encouragement and ideas. His support extended beyond what most chief psychologists are able to give. To Dr. John Cody, I am grateful for all the help and encouragement I received while working at the High Plains Comprehensive Community Mental Health Center (Hays, Kansas). I would also like to thank Dr. Jerome S. Kutner, who was the first master teacher of psychology I ever experienced; and Dr. Jim Ryabik, who was an important teacher and colleague.

I am indebted to Virginia Satir, who taught me, among other things, how to conceptualize stress reactions. Also, Dr. Tom Gordon provided valuable insights into viewing verbal interaction as a tool that can be understood and utilized. Dr. Tom Gordon also taught me principles concerning the notion of problem ownership. These concepts have become universalized, but Dr. Gordon originated these ideas.

My gratitude also goes to the people who have contributed directly to the preparation of this book. Judy Manka, Sharon Bowles, Patrick Schniederjan, June Bachus and Sam Sackett all provided a considerable amount of encouragement, support and ideas that are deeply appreciated. I would also like to express my gratitude to Rebecka Stucky for her critique of the manuscript. And I am deeply indebted to Darren Liby, who cheerfully contributed his artistic abilities in the development of the charts and illustrations.

TABLE OF CONTENTS

CHAPTER		Page
I	A TIME FOR REMEMBERING	1
	Looking Back	5
	From Whence We Came.	5
	First Influence.	6
	Second Influence.	7
	Third Influence	8
II	PERCEPTIONS, FEELINGS AND BEHAVIOR	13
	The Perceptual Experience	14
	Maslow's Hierarchy	18
	A Word of Caution	27
	Perceptions and Feelings.	32
	Behavior	43
	A Word on Behavior	47
III	HANDLING STRESS	50
	Interpersonal Stress.	50
	Conversational Listening.	53
	Active Listening	54
	For Parents and Teachers: Handling Stressful Situations	60
	Interaction with Positive Consequences.	63
	Interaction with Negative Consequences	64
	Some Cautions	66
IV	TEACHING EMOTIONAL EDUCATION IN THE CLASSROOM	67
	Grade Levels and Goals.	70
	First Grade Activities	72
	Naming Feelings	72
	Homework	72
	Group Dictionaries	73

CHAPTER		Page
IV	(Continued)	

First Grade Activities (continued)
Short Narratives 74
Getting Big 74
Second Grade Activities 75
Feelings and Behavior 75
Feelings and Behavior (second session) . . .77
Put-ups and Put-downs 79
Stories. 80
Being a Friend. .81
Inside-Outside. .81
Simon Feels. 82
Faces. 83
Decks of Cards .84
Chip Trading. 85
Cupped Puppetry: Approaching
People. 85
Third Grade Activities. 87
Strengthening "Feelings and
Behavior" 87
Behavior Analysis 87
Cory and Kim 87
A Picture Dictionary for Third
Grade Students 88
Being a Friend. .89
Discovering 89
Known and Unknown Friends. 90
Skitting It 92
Meg. 93
Feelings and Behavior Bank. 94
Picture Stories. .95
Fourth Grade Activities. 96
Coffee Cups, Chairs or Whatever 96
The Gossip Game 98
Perceptions and Feelings and
Behaviors. 98
Perceptions and Feelings and
Behaviors (second session). 100

IV   (Continued)
          Fourth Grade Activities (continued)
              Perceptions and Feelings Bank 103
              Being a Friend. 104
              Put ups and Put downs 104
              Perceptions and Behavior Bank 105
              Changing Positions 106
              Known and Unknown Friends. 109
              Simon Perceives. 109
              Short Stories. .110
              Behavior Analysis and Alternatives 110
          Fifth Grade Activities 110
              Interpersonal Consequences 110
              A Throw of Dice. 112
              Short Narratives 114
                  Bob and Tom 114
                  Tina and Carol. 115
              Seizing the Teachable Moment 115
              Previous Activities. 117
              Inclusion and Exclusion 117
              Inclusion and Exclusion Follow-up 118
              Perceptions and Consequences Bank 119
              Imports and Exports. 121
              Conversational Listening. 122
          Sixth Grade Activities. 124
              Previous Learnings. 124
              Languaging:
                  First Session 124
                  Second Session 125
                  Third Session. 127
                  Fourth Session 127
                  Fifth Session 128
                  Sixth Session. 128
                  Seventh Session. 129
              Utilizing Communication Skills. 130
                  Space Journey. 130
                  Out at Sea. 131
                  Family: Plan Something 132

   IV   (Continued)

          Sixth Grade Activities (continued)

             Real Issues. 132

                Attention vs. Acceptance 132

          Secondary Level Activities 133

             Course I. 133

                Unfinished Business. 133

                How many. 133

                Shades. 134

                Chains. 134

                Changing Perceptions 136

                Hearing: Feeling Starting and

                    Feeling Stopping. 137

                Court. 139

                Interpretations 140

                Behavior: Satisfying Feelings and

                    Considering Consequences. 142

                Role Playing Not Listening 143

                Hearing Names 143

              Course II. 144

                Dynamics of Perceptions. 144

                Rejection: Its Pain and Its Effects. . .145

                Climbing .146

                Changing Positions 147

                Inclusion and Exclusion 147

                Self-Concept: Its Causes and

                    Its Effects 147

                Attribution 149

                Active Listening 151

              Course III 155

                Typical Reactions to Stress. 155

                Assuming Positions 155

                Handling Stress: Who, if anyone,

                    Owns the Problem. 156

                When Other Person Owns Problem . .157

                When You Own The Problem 159

                Parenting and Teaching. 160

REFERENCES 165

CHAPTER I

A TIME FOR REMEMBERING

Cold-Fingers was a man who understood the problems his village was having. Although he was obviously a leader within the community, some people considered him to be out of step with the rest of the people in the village. To some, he seemed hopelessly preoccupied with looking for ways of making life easier. Some villagers felt that Cold-Fingers should just accept life as the way it was since there was no way of really changing that way of life. Besides that, their lifestyle had been deeply rooted in tradition and customs that had been handed down for generations. And, like many people, these villagers resisted an alteration of lifelong practices and beliefs.

Cold-Fingers and his peers lived at a time when the earth was cold. Hugh sheets of ice, called glaciers, spread out from the North Pole and the South Pole, and from the high mountains. As far as Cold-Fingers and his peers knew, the frozen plains and sub-zero temperatures which surrounded the village represented a way of life that never had, and never would, change.

Many animals also lived on these icy, cold plains. There were big, ferocious cave bears. There was also cave leopards and cave lions, but it was the cave bears that struck fear into the hearts of Cold-Fingers and the other villagers. Frequently, the bears entered the village, especially when they were hungry. If the cave bears were not able to find enough food to satisfy their appetites, it was not unusual for a villager to lose his life as victim to these man-eating bears.

Other animals that helped meet the most basic needs of the people also lived on these plains. There was the giant elk, a beautiful creature more than six feet high. Its antlers were huge and heavy, like great, spreading tree branches. Even though the elk were top heavy with their huge antlers, they were quite fast. But when the villagers were fortunate enough to capture one of these animals, they enjoyed a feast that was considered a delicacy to all. And there was the slow, plodding mammoth of the plains. The mammoths had shaggy, reddish-brown hair. The wooly skins of the great mammoth provided warmth for the people of Cold-Finger's village. But one had to be extremely cautious in capturing these animals. Although these animals were plant-eaters, their great curled tusks could be quite dangerous, especially if they were cornered.

As it happened, these animals provided the subject area for the curriculum of the first school the village ever had. Cold-Fingers clearly perceived three primary problems facing his village: food, clothing and the attack of the always hungry cave bear. He had seen far too many villagers become victims of starvation, freezing and the flesh-eating bear. Not only was Cold-Fingers interested in doing something about these problems today, but when his children were grown, he wanted them to have more to eat, more skins to keep warm and to be free of danger of the cave bear.

Having set up these educational goals, Cold-Fingers proceeded to create a method for obtaining these goals. He established the village's first educational curriculum. In constructing the curriculum, he was aware of the delicious meat that the elk provided. He also knew the elk were quite fast and they also had a keen sense of hearing. One could not outrun the elk. And it was next to impossible to sneak up on them. The few times that either of these methods worked were lucky — and rare. So Cold-Fingers talked to Full-Belly, the only one in the entire village who had more than his share of luck at elk-catching. He learned that Full-Belly had devised an ingenious snare to catch the elk by the antlers as they sped through the forest portion of the plains. Full-Belly agreed to share his ideas with other villagers so they could also enjoy Full-Belly's prosperity.

And Cold-Fingers put forth the first subject of the first curriculum: elk-snaring. To make the course more complete, Full-Belly also agreed to share the knowledge he had on how to weave and build snares. The snare must be strong enough to hold the powerful elk. Full-Belly was the teacher.

Cold-Fingers continued his thinking. He knew the mammoth skins were by far the best way to keep warm during the freezing temperatures that seemed to always be with them. But there just weren't enough skins to go around. So Cold-Fingers talked to Warm-Feet. Somehow Warm-Feet always seemed to have an ample supply of skins and furs to provide warmth for his family and friends. He found out Warm-Feet's secret. He learned that part of the plains was the mammoth's regular "territory" and that each mammoth staked out its own path as it moved from place to place. Warm-Feet had developed a way of tracking the mammoths, and it was a very unique way of trapping them. Shallow pits were the most effective way of trapping these animals. Surprisingly, these mammoths could not climb out of a trap that was three feet high. But the shallow holes must have enough length and width in order to assure the animal's capture.

So mammoth-tracking-and-hole-digging was added as the second subject in the new curriculum. Warm-Feet was the teacher.

Finally, Cold-Fingers talked to Smart-Trap about his unusual but effective way of trapping the cave bear. He found that deep and narrow pits were the best way of trapping the bear, but the bears were clever enough to make this a tricky operation. The pits had to be camouflaged in a very careful manner or else the bear would simply avoid the pits. And the size of the pits was of crucial importance. They had to be big enough to capture the bear but if the width and depth were oversized, the bear could detect the camouflage and simply avoid the pits.

Thus, Cold-Fingers developed the third subject: pit-making-and-camouflaging-for-the-cave-bear. Smart-Trap was the teacher.

A new era had emerged. The first school had been developed. What more could you want? All the conditions to form a flawless "match" between the community and the school had been shaped by Cold-Fingers. The curriculum was designed to meet the needs of the people within the community. It was truly an "ice-age" curriculum. Everyone prospered. The students were excited about learning and the citizens were better fed, better clothed and safer than ever before. Times were never so good. And it was all due to the ability and willingness of the school to blend the learning activities of the students in unison with what the students needed to learn.

As generations passed, times changed. The icy cold temperatures had been replaced by a warmer climate. The glaciers had disappeared. Many of the animals that used to roam the ice age plains had also vanished. The wooly mammoths had become extinct. The giant elk and the cave bear had moved to the north, staying with the sub-zero temperatures they were so well adapted to.

Over a period of time, the school had found itself in a very difficult situation. Even though there were no longer any elk to share, the course was still being taught in the schools. Although the mammoths had become extinct, mammoth-tracking-and-hole-digging remained as a required subject in the school's curriculum. There had not been one reported sighting of a cave bear for years, even generations, but pit-making-and-camouflaging-for-the-cave-bear was still a "basic" part of the students' coursework. Although the plains were now warm, even hot in the summer, the "ice-age" curriculum was still being taught in the schools.

The attitude of the students had also changed. As the "basics" became more and more removed from the needs of the students and community, the excitement of learning gave way to other attitudes. Suddenly, the schools were confronted with a set of attitudes they had never before encountered: discipline problems, attitude problems and attendance problems. The villagers wondered, "What went wrong?"

In the spirit of Cold-Fingers, a group of radicals approached the village council to suggest a need to update the school's curriculum. The radicals argued that there was a need to adapt what was being taught in the schools to new problems that the people were encountering. They argued, "If we can't change what is being taught altogether, why can't we at least add to the curriculum to help us meet some of today's problems?"

The council's response was predictable — disappointing, but predictable. They smiled at the group of young radicals in a very fatherly manner and said, "Elk-snaring, mammoth-trapping and cave-bear trapping are *basics*. We can't change these standardized fundamentals." The council went on to argue that the frills that the radicals wanted to move into the curriculum wouldn't be *education*. Besides, the argument continued, the school curriculum is too crowded with what we have now. We can't add more. As for the discipline problems, the village council suggested that the schools adapt a new "get tough" policy. A rigid corporal punishment regime was recommended.

Looking Back:
      In hindsight, we can clearly perceive that the nature of the problems that the descendants of Cold-Fingers faced were different than the ones that contributed to the "ice-age" curriculum. In retrospect, the contrast is quite distinct. But the unfolding of the new and different set of circumstances that the villagers learned to cope with was so gradual that one could only dimly perceive the evolution as it was occurring. Slowly and imperceptibly, the foundation and the reason for the school's existence was eroded away. That erosion was so gradual it was extremely difficult to adapt to the changes as they were occurring. Finally, education was stripped of its meaning and its appeal because of an inability to keep up with the times. The passage of time cast a new shadow over our schools, and the schools just failed to grasp its meaning. In essence, the problem is that education is a fragile commodity that can be easily depleted as a resource if it is no longer useful to the community or to the students. And the village council didn't understand that basic premise.

From Whence We Came:
      In hindsight, Cold-Fingers' descendants found themselves in a very unfortunate situation. New ideas not allowed to infiltrate the curriculum and the schools eventually lost their meaning and relevance. We cannot afford to make the same mistake. We, the schools, cannot ask something of the students that we are unable to give—to adjust to the times. To be sure, we have not yet arrived at the position at which the group of young

5

radicals who faced the village council found themselves. It is too early to tell if we will ever arrive at the same state of affairs—where the needs of the community and students are so completely polarized from what the school is teaching. But we are moving in that direction. In order for education to continue as a viable and useful resource, we, as educators, must be more adaptable than the village council. If we look at the history of education and some of the influences that have helped to shape education, some trends become alarmingly clear.

First Influence

Aristotle's teacher, Plato, had a tremendous impact on education. To be sure, in comparison to Aristotle, Plato's influence was small. Plato's disciple could hardly be matched for influence on the world he left behind. Yet Plato also had a distinct impact.

The revolutionary spirit of educational reform ran parallel to Plato's life. It began around 400 B.C. and, like all reform, represented an attempt to make strides toward "progress."

On the one hand, Plato's thinking proved to be very modern and up-to-date. He recognized that education had the potential to be one of the central sources of influence on a community's values and attitudes. In other words, for Plato, the teaching of facts and raw information was not enough. There must be more. Otherwise our academicism may be keen but personal qualities would suffer. To be maximally effective, we must teach the "total" student.

Obviously, the educational reform, led by Plato's influence, had many honorable and modern goals. But there were serious inconsistencies as well. Plato was interested in educating an elite corps in order to form a strong, but narrow, base of community strength. Plato was so intent on achieving his worthwhile goals that the means of obtaining those ends became obfuscated. In attempting to expedite community leadership in intellectual and emotional areas, he seemed to forget the very objective he sought to obtain. For example, he also subjugated the students to the state:

"But every 'man-Jack' of them (as the saying goes)

must, so far as possible, be compelled to be educated, inasmuch as they are children of the state, even more than of their parents."

Through Plato's influence, not only were teachers appointed as guardians of the children's education for the first time on a regular basis, but he was also the architect of what became one of our most powerful social institutions. Plato was much like Cold-Fingers. Through his influence, teachers were appointed and schools were developed. In addition to Plato's interest in the expediency of learning, one could also detect a subtle, but ever pervasive, attitude toward the learning process itself. Increased learning? Appointing teachers? No one would quarrel with these worthwhile goals and methods. But did Plato go too far?

Second Influence

The second major influence took place with the advent of the printing press. The impact was immediate. Learning to read and write became more important than ever before. All of a sudden, the written word was relied upon heavily by a majority of people as a way of transmitting information on a daily, routine basis. In fact, the printed word was relied upon so heavily in our society, that considerable time and energy were spent learning how to read and write. The emphasis in our schools began to shift from transmitting ideas and information to the acquisition of the "basic" skills. Actually, reading and writing became "basics" in our schools as a response to our students' needs.

A new era had begun. A major educational revolution was now underway. Students could learn more than ever before. And it also proved that education was capable of adapting its curriculum to the changing times—at least in those instances in which that transition could be understood.

But there were other, more indistinct, consequences that also began to emerge. The new "basics" began to give rise to these unforeseen effects. As people relied more heavily upon the written word as a method of communication, verbal communication became less important. Thus, at least one hard to distinguish impact of this new phenomenon was the beginning of a gradual erosion of the need for verbal communication and interaction among people.

Third Influence

We are experiencing the third major influence at the present time. The explosion in the utilization of the electronic media is having a major impact on all our lives. Now, learning is easier, more efficient, and more complete than it ever has been. Our students know more information about a variety of subjects than any of our ancestors would have dreamed possible. Our students' level of awareness about so many topics is at the highest level in history. No wonder. Radio and television have enabled us to exchange ideas and information with minimal effort on the part of the learner.

As one might anticipate, times have changed since the advent of the printing press. After all, the very nature of the method of our learning has been altered. But that alteration has not changed our ideas about what our students need, or about what are the "basics." Thus, while it is true that the boom in electronics has resulted in an unparalleled ability to massively communicate ideas and intelligent data, this has also created a central paradox in education. That is, a reduction of our dependence on the "basics" has been the result of the rapid and easy learning that has burst forth.

Our heavy reliance upon reading and writing for the passage of information has diminished. It hasn't disappeared but it has diminished. We still need these basic skills for job related skills, whether it is reading professional material or filling out job application forms. And many people still read for entertainment. But nightly news broadcasts are relied upon at an increasingly high rate. More people rely upon television and radio than newspapers. We don't NEED newspapers to pass along information as we once did. More and more, newspapers are thought of as a secondary resource in obtaining information.

In math, calculators are helping us solve problems that, just a few years ago, were left to our own computational skills. In the not too distant past, any math problem that needed solution had to be hand-calculated. But, again, times have changed. These gadgets have replaced the old pencil and paper calculation with a speed and accuracy that had never been known to most people.

And there is the tiny electronic computer engraved on a silicon chip which is at the heart of the personal computer revolution. That microprocessor has been able to put power into the hands of neophytes that was once only available in gigantic mainframe computers run by experts in the field. The impact of all the software, display screens, disc drives and printers associated with the personal computer is incomprehensible. One thing is certain: no longer is the computer's power available only to a technocratic elite. The widespread dispersal of these amazing devices is certain to have a profound impact on us all. There can be little doubt that we are experiencing the third revolution at the present time.

Now, a word of caution. It would be a serious mistake to take the position that the traditional "basics," as defined by reading and math, are no longer needed. Reading is still an important and vital skill. So is math. Actually, we will always need these skills. But the emphasis is shifting. We need to be aware of these changes so we can adjust our curriculum accordingly.

Actually, it is difficult not to applaud the achievements of what "basic" learning has brought. Obviously, it is not the intent to suggest that reading books and watching Sesame Street are evils that need to be eradicated. No way. Many positive gains in the development of our children and in our society can be attributed to these influences. But we do need to be wary of the total impact of these influences so that we can compensate for otherwise worthwhile accomplishments. We do not need to throw the curriculum out. We need to enhance it. What we need to enhance it with must begin with a crystal clear perspective of what is involved in our students' learning and educational experiences.

One of the more indistinct consequences has been a gradual erosion of the human or subjective element from the educational process. With our increased ability to absorb more and more information, and to solve problems of a more complex nature, we can detect a greater emphasis on "being right."

Concomitant with this gradual emphasis of rightfulness has been a heightened apprehension of being "wrong."

New criteria are continually emerging to assist educators in measuring students' learning. We are constantly arriving at higher levels of development in order to help us evaluate the amount of knowledge a student is learning as well as the acquisition of basic skills. These standards have become more and more objective. And, as we have elevated objectivity to an increasingly lofty status, other imperceptible attitudes have evolved. That is, a rejection of the subjective factor has moved in tandem with our quest for objectivity. Presently, anything subjective, such as feelings and personal thoughts, has not been allowed to infiltrate our search for knowledge and for more "basics." There is not enough room in our already jampacked curriculum for such frills as our children's social and emotional development.

Generations and generations of these attitudes have had a definite impact on our students' relationships with one another. "Understanding" has taken on a new meaning. To "understand" is to observe, classify and categorize in a very objective, judgmental manner. In a very subtle and implicit way, this has contributed to a system of behavioral dualism of being "right or wrong," of "winning or losing," of "good or bad."

This system of behavioral dualism has contributed to a method of thinking *and* interacting that goes beyond academic and achievement implications. The ramifications touch the social and emotional development of our students as well. It has established a method interacting that fails to explain or understand — only classify. Thus:

GOOD	BAD
independent	dependent
normal	abnormal
rich	poor
healthy	disabled
same	different

and in men

strong	weak
aggressive	timid
insensitive	sensitive

GOOD		BAD
industrious		without a job
	and in women	
weak		strong
sensitive		insensitive
timid		aggressive
without a job		industrious
	and in children	
dependent		independent
high grades		low grades
obedient		disobedient
quiet		talkative or disruptive

Many of the perceptions and feelings students have about themselves *and* others are generated by these attitudes. Many of these attitudes come from school-related experiences. And yes, this approach to personal relationships and social interaction does have a significant impact in the emotional and social development of our students.

Look around. On the one hand, you see high technology producing gee-whiz gadgetry at a dazzling speed. The computerized technologies with all the circuitry and silicon chips are advancing at an accelerated rate. Yet, in spite of all of our knowledge and job related competence, the Ford Foundation found that 80% of *all* people fired at *all* job levels are not fired because of a lack of job knowledge or job competency. Rather, the vast majority of people who do not succeed in their chosen field can attribute their failure to an inability to relate effectively with other people. Look around. You will see mounting social problems and very real human problems in spite of bountiful knowledge, information and technology.

Alarmingly, there are as many new psychiatric patients being admitted to our clinics as there are full-time college freshmen enrolling in all our colleges and universities. There are many other social problems on the dramatic rise. Tragic stories could be told about the suicides which number between thirty and one hundred thousand each year, or the alcoholics, the juvenile delinquents, the drug abusers, divorces and day-to-day emotional pain that we all experience.

Actually, a whole book could be written on only one

phase of our social problems—child abuse. Four million incidents of child abuse or neglect occur every year in these United States. Ten thousand children are severely battered. Two thousand are killed by their parents for not "behaving." The list could go on and on. But all you have to do is look around. Look at the schools. Look at the playgrounds. Problems are mounting at an alarming pace: discipline problems, attitude problems, attendance problems, motivational problems and, that's right, delinquency problems. And now, we are wondering "What went wrong?"

Obvious parallels could be drawn between the educational and social conditions that existed during the post "ice-age" era with conditions that exist at the present time. But there are significant differences as well. Our present day "basics" are still an integral part of the skills that are needed in order to cope effectively in our culture. However, as our "human" problems continue to escalate, there is a corresponding need to understand that our "basics" must evolve and not become stagnant.

Can we do any more than the village council who faced the descendants of Cold-Fingers as they tried to blend current educational practices with the needs of the people? Just what can we do?

CHAPTER II

PERCEPTIONS, FEELINGS AND BEHAVIOR

There is a central question that underlies the entire book: Is it possible for basic psychological principles to be taught effectively in the classroom on a regular basis with teachers and/ or counselors acting as instructors and facilitators? Yes, most definitely. So long as the approach that is used is sufficiently clear and teachable so that: (1) Teachers and counselors feel comfortable using it as a tool; (2) It is applicable to *all* children and not merely a few "distrubed" students; and (3) It is not *only* taught as a special set of instructional material but is integrated into other phases of the regular school experience. For example, we all know *who* discovered America and *when* it was discovered, but we usually don't go beyond names and events. Very little, if any, time has been spent trying to discover *why* Columbus set forth on his adventure. Few students have tried to guess some of the feelings that Columbus may have had that caused him to set sail. Most students fail to understand that Columbus was a human being who had certain motivations and strivings and that the discovery of America was a consequence of the way one person handled his feelings. We fail to recognize some possible consequences if Columbus would have done something else to handle those same feelings.

The integration of these psychological principles must go beyond curricular instruction. In order to be maximally effective, these psychological understandings must also guide the manner in which we interact with students, both in the type of situation in which discipline is needed, and in those conditions in which praise, reinforcement and encouragement may be needed. The next chapter deals with these "how to" issues.

The Perceptual Experience

Perception is defined as the awareness, or the process of becoming aware, of the outside world as it relates to the individual. This is affected by our senses and is under the influence of our personal resources, psychological need states and, obviously, the external world as it exists. It is usually extremely difficult to distinguish the perceptual event from these influences as well as from the associations, memories and feelings that also feed into our perception of a given situation.

One primary characteristic of our perceptual experience rests in the dynamic quality of those experiences. Because our perceptual experiences are being influenced by so many sources, they are continually changing and are marked by continuous fluctuations. And those dynamics involve internal as well as external cues.

This is characteristic of our perceptual experience. Every time we perceive anything at all, we focus on a perceptual *"figure"* that stands out from the general back*ground*. Quite often we experience fluctuations in our perceptions without even being aware of those changes. Our perceptual "figure" and "ground" shifts and our focus of attention changes. In general, our perceptual "figure" has a recognizable shape, while what is "ground" does not. We attend to a given "figure" and everything else simply fades away into oblivion. Figure 1 shows how this works.

In Figure 1, you can either see a black goblet as a perceptual "figure" that is standing in front of a white "ground," or you can see two white faces looking at each other in front of a black 'ground." If you think you see both at the same time, you really don't. You are probably either alternating between the two or you see one region of the contour as part of the white profile and another as part of the black vase.

We all experience a dynamic figure-ground relationship that is constantly changing. If you are listening to the music of the stereo, the music is the figure of your perception; the baseball game across the street is in the ground. But if you were a school-age youngster listening to the stereo and were wonder-

14

FIGURE 1

ing why you weren't invited to join in, your personal sense of rejection and feelings of sadness could well be the "figure" of your experiences and the stereo would be in the background. Or suppose you are listening to the music and the phone suddenly rings. Your attention focuses on the phone; it becomes the figure, and you rise to answer it as the music recedes into the ground. You conduct your conversation on the phone. Now the sound of a siren outside your window claims the figure of your awareness. Momentarily, the telephone becomes less important. Perhaps a fear swelling up inside becomes the focus of your consciousness, especially if you imagine a close friend having had an accident.

When we observe students "having trouble concentrating" or "resisting learning," this is essentially what we are seeing. A student who cannot concentrate on the assignment as the perceptual figure could well be experiencing such fluctuations of the "figure" and "ground."

And now the hitch! If it were only as simple as alternating perception, it would be much easier. While it is true that we do focus on a perceptual "figure," and the background sort of fades away, many hidden elements of the "ground" influence our perceptual experiences in ways that are outside our awareness. Our perception of any given situation is never "pure." Figure 2 shows how our perception of a given "figure" may be unconsciously affected by forces within the "ground." For instance, if you were asked "Which figure is the largest, the man or the boy?" what would your response be?

Actually, if you measure both heights with a ruler, you will find them to be the same size. What happened? Factors affected your perception of a situation that were outside your level of immediate awareness. Can you identify what factors influenced your perception?

Real life social situations are much more confusing and ambiguous than experiments with points and lines. Facial expressions, tones of voice, the direction of another person's gaze, and the size of a social group are only a tiny portion of the total number of possible elements of a situation that affect our perception. That's not all. Our own ability, or lack thereof, to cope with any given social situation also plays very heavily on our perception of that situation. Our underlying physical

FIGURE 2

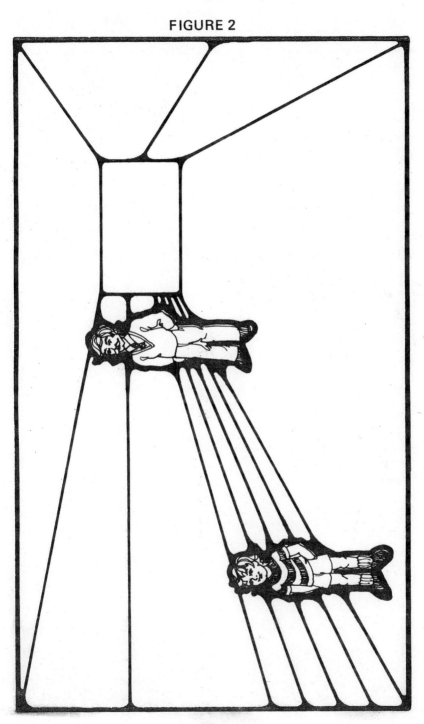

and psychological need states are also very important as we attempt to perceive any given situation. Thus, there are at least three sets of circumstances or characteristics that could contribute to variability in our perceptions of other people and social situations: (1) Psychological need states that the person might be experiencing (Maslow); (2) The environmental situation as it actually exists; and (3) The personal resources that the person feels he has in coping with the situation as perceived.

Abraham Maslow (1954) set forth some concepts that seem especially helpful as we consider some of the factors that influence our perceptual experiences in social situations. Mas-. low felt that people have five psychological need states. These needs are not all equally urgent; some are more basic than others. Because of this inequality, they can be arranged in order from the most basic to the least. Even the least basic is a legitimate life force, but it cannot be attended to until the others have been satisfactorily met.

The psychological needs are:

(1) *Physiological needs.* These are the most basic of all human needs; they include food, warmth, shelter, water, elimination, sleep and other bodily needs.

(2) *Safety needs.* These are the demands for physical safety, feelings of being safe from injury, both physical and emotional, as well as the absence of fear for one's safety.

(3) *Need for belongingness and love.* This represents the first social need. This is the need for other people; to feel a part of, and to belong to, someone else.

(4) *Self-esteem needs.* A person has a basic need for self-respect and the esteem of others. This includes both the need for feeling a personal worth, adequacy and competence *as well as* the need for respect, admiration and status in the eyes of others.

(5) *Self-actualization needs.* These include the need to function at a high level of performance, to achieve mastery over an area to the

fullest degree possible and to "become" as competent as one is able.

Until one need is fulfilled, a person's behavior is not motivated by the next higher need. Maslow's theory postulates the first four needs as *deficit* needs, as they serve to motivate and stimulate a person in their absence, or because of a deficit. One strives for fulfillment of each successive level of the first four steps because of a *lack* of food, a *lack* of safety, a *lack* of love and a *lack* of self-esteem.

As we consider the figure-ground aspect of our perceptual experiences, this becomes even clearer. That is, the perceptual "figure" of a person remains at the level of whatever need is the most basic that is not being met. One simply cannot focus his attention to the next higher level until the more primitive need has been met. This is intuitively obvious. If we hadn't eaten in the last twenty-four hours, it would be very difficult for us to try to concentrate on a homework assignment, at least until we had something to eat. Until that happened, our total perceptual experience would be wrapped up in our hunger. Figure 3 shows how our psychological need states influence our perceptions.

This has created an unfortuate hiatus. Emphasis on academic production assumes that students are ready for exercises in self-actualization. With very few exceptions, our students' first three psychological needs are being met quite adequately within the home. That is as it should be because the family impacts most upon the three most basic needs.

Actually, all this seems satisfactory. Where is the rub? The problem is self-esteem, or self-concept. Since self-esteem is mostly defined by one's peer group, the family has little impact on this need. The schools do not include the building of self-esteem as a part of their instructional experiences for two reasons. Adequate tools to deal with this crucial need have not been supplied. Most of what students receive in this area is "hit and miss." And, you might add, the schools are under ample pressure to produce more "basics."

We must recognize that a child is a member of two worlds: the world of adults and the world of his peers. His experience in each of these worlds is vitally important in mold-

FIGURE 3

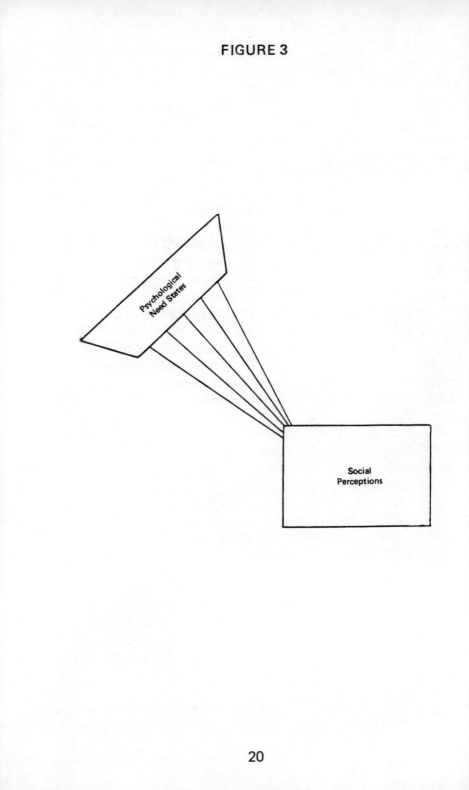

ing *different* needs in the child's social and psychological development. Psychological research points out that early in a child's group and classroom experience, the peers form an impression of that child. On the basis of those impressions, the child is assigned a group status that is amazingly stable over time. The evidence is clear that once children have been assigned that status, it is very difficult to alter those impressions or that status. Probably one of the most crucial functions of those peer relationships and "assignments" is the manner in which the group helps the child form his self-concept. Early in group experiences, the child becomes aware that his peers place him in particular categories and, as the child matures in age, he becomes increasingly sensitive to that implicit assignment. That cumulative assignment by his peers exerts a powerful influence over the way the child perceives himself. This is directly related to the building of self-esteem.

There is no doubt that family relationships are the primary architects of human relationships. The principle agent for transmitting culturally determined values and attitudes is the family. And the role of the family extends well beyond that of cultural mediator. The fact is that we, as educators, must depend upon the home to meet the three most basic needs of our students. However, the world of adults does *not* extend into the world of the child where self-concept and self-esteem are rooted so deeply in their day-to-day interactions. As Maslow's hierarchy of needs would suggest, it is true that a child's self-esteem would suffer if the need for love and belonging were not met. But we cannot assume that meeting the child's need for love will have any direct effect on self-esteem.

By default, the development of self-esteem is left to chance. On the one hand, the family's influence over these critical peer group interactions, which forms the basis of self-esteem, is minimal. On the other hand, those adults who are in a position to make some inroads in this crucial area of child development are helpless. Although educators are fully sensitive to these problems, precious little time in education is assigned for implementation in the classroom. Educators have no tools to work with.

It should be of no major surprise that an abundance of psychological research points to "self-concept" as a major

21

problem facing our students today. Just what does that mean? There are a variety of implications. Since self-esteem is a more basic need than self-actualization, many of our students are not experiencing enough degrees of freedom to focus their full energy on self-actualization. Thus, they are not achieving up to their "potential." Instead of concentrating fully on schoolwork, a significant amount of their resources is spent focusing on an unmet need. And if the need for self-esteem is blocked, it may show up in unexpected ways. In some cases, the perceptual figure of a person may involve that unmet need. That creates a certain amount of personal stress. Everything else, including academic and social skills, would be relegated to the background. The perceptual "figure" could be feelings of stress that are attached to a loss of self-esteem. It is at times like these that the reasons for a person's behavior are not readily apparent. We can't observe what the person is responding to. We don't understand the behavior that we see.

* * * * * * * * * *

Duane left fifteen minutes early for school. When he left, he was feeling in a good mood. His parents cared for him very much and, in all, were very good parents. He was lucky to have such a good family. Duane knew all this. Yet somehow, he never had been able to be "one of the gang." He always felt on the perimeter of being one of "the group."

Duane usually left early for school. That way he didn't have to face the emotional hurt of not being asked to walk with everyone else. But today he had forgotten about the class meeting that was being held before school. As he walked out the door, he saw three classmates walking together. When they saw Duane, they crossed the street so they could avoid being close to him. Still further down the street, another group of classmates, this time four in number, walked right past him. They acted as if they didn't even see him.

At the class meeting, the teacher asked the class to decide whether they wanted a class party to be a skating party or to go out for pizza. The teacher really wanted some discussion on the matter. When no one volunteered an opinion, she asked Duane for an opinion—just to get the discussion going. But Duane was still deeply hurt from the earlier experiences. Instead of getting the discussion going, the teacher noticed a tear

22

rolling down Duane's cheek. His self-esteem was shattered.

* * * * * * * * * *

At the time of the meeting, Duane's perceptual figure was his own sense of lost self-esteem. As Maslow indicated, self-esteem is a deficit need that is activated by its absence. The more one feels without it, there is an increasing tendency to focus more and more attention upon it. And no one in class ever knew what was bothering Duane—even the classmates who contributed to the problem. After all, they didn't "do" anything. His disrupted self-esteem represented his perceptual figure throughout the class discussion. All his teacher and classmates observed was his lack of interest in the party, and the fact that something was bothering him. It is at times like these that the reasons for a person's behavior are not readily apparent. We can't observe what the person is responding to and, therefore, we don't understand that behavior.

But the lack of self-esteem, or any other psychological need, doesn't always have to be the "figure" of one's perception. It can be much more complex than that. Our lack of self-esteem can also strongly influence our feelings and behavior even if it isn't the primary driving force in our perceptual experiences. Just like in Figure 2, where the background cues obfuscated a clear perception of what we were trying to see, our own lack of self-esteem can creep into our perceptual field and affect us in funny little ways that are outside our level of awareness.

Another important factor that influences our perception of any given situation is, obviously, the external environment. Actually, many factors within any given environmental situation have an impact on our perceptions. Just like some of the factors that affected our perception in Figure 2 (page 17), some of the influences are outside our awareness. If you're driving around town and notice that the fuel gauge registers "half," you tend to read it as half full. But if you're heading toward an open highway on a weekend—particularly if you have had difficulty buying gasoline on weekends—your perception changes. The same half-full tank is now half-empty. That altered perception will affect the way you feel and behave.

Previous experiences that we have encountered in our environment distinctly influence our perceptions. Repeated

23

failures or astounding successes in school may result in a person emotionally accepting a certain evaluation of his or her ability to learn in school. Previous experiences also affects us in other areas, such as in sports or in interpersonal relationships. For instance, if a child isn't invited to birthday parties, or if no one asks that child to spend the night when that is the "in" thing to do, or if no one wants to walk to school with the child, these could all have an impact upon a person's perceptions. Comments by parents, siblings, peers and various authorities can bind a person to some particular idea. It may be that he isn't bright enough to learn, or that his ability lies in only one area, or that he can't play tennis. In early childhood, a parent may have said repeatedly, "You certainly are hopeless in arithmetic." Failing marks and a seeming inability to keep up with friends—a variety of things have an impact upon a person's perception of how he relates to his environment.

In fact, the number of external influences on our perceptions is almost immeasurable. The place of our residence, the fraternity we belong to, the clubs we are associated with, our professional position, the way our colleague looks at us during coffee break, the car we drive, the television show we are watching, the clothes we wear, all have a bearing on the manner in which we perceive ourselves within our environment. Figure 4 shows how the environment affects our perceptions.

* * * * * * * * * *

Jamie was talking to her sister about a problem she was having at school. Jamie's sister, Susie, was getting poor marks in a geography course. Jamie had taken the course the year before and had passed the course. Susie was hoping that Jamie could help her prepare for a test she was taking tomorrow. But as Susie was explaining her problem to Jamie, all Jamie could think about was *her* boyfriend and the way he seemed to avoid her in school that day. Jamie couldn't concentrate on Susie. Soon Susie became acutely aware that her sister wasn't listening to her problems.

* * * * * * * * * *

This was a typical clash of perceptions of two people that were unwilling, or unable, to listen to one another. Both Jamie and Susie were relegating each other to the background in favor of their own, individual "figure." In this case, something that

FIGURE 4

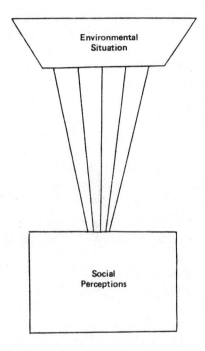

had just happened was interfering with Jamie's ability to allow her sister into her perceptual figure. Just as likely, our perceptions may be affected by some future event.

* * * * * * * * * *

Brad was an average student. He received passing grades in all courses that he was taking. He received much of his satisfaction and rewards from his basketball playing ability. He played on the varsity squad and, for a sophomore, he was doing quite well. Even though Brad was taking an exam that afternoon, he seemed to be more aware of the basketball game to be played that night. His thoughts kept drifting to the game. He was rehearsing some of the plays the team had practiced. The exam, and Brad's thoughts about the exam, crept further and further into the background.

* * * * * * * * * *

There is at least one other aspect that affects our perceptual field. Those are the personal resources that we carry to any given situation. We are not equal in our native ability to do well in various and different tasks, whether they are intellectual or athletic in nature—or in any given activity.

* * * * * * * * * *

Jeff and Steve were walking by the playground. They noticed several boys were playing basketball, as they often did on Saturday afternoons. The boys playing basketball asked Jeff and Steve to play with them. Steve, being a good basketball player, became very excited and his attention focused immediately on the game and his chance "to shine." Jeff, somewhat shorter than the other players and rather clumsy when it came to basketball, became keenly aware of his admitted poor skills. His perceptual figure was not the basketball game but a self-consciousness about his own inability.

* * * * * * * * * *

Linda had never been a good student. Her classmates knew of the problems she had in learning because her name was usually at the bottom of the list when it came time to post test scores. Nor only were Linda's test performances below the class norm, but when asked a question in class, Linda never seemed able to represent her point of view very well. She was bright enough, but when it came to academics, Linda always seemed to take a back seat. She realized the problem she had in school and whenever she entered the classroom—especially math—she felt overwhelmed by a sense of inadquacy.

*   *   *   *   *   *   *   *   *   *

This is characteristic of our perceptual experience. Every time we perceive anything at all, we focus on something that stands out from the general back*ground*. Thus, one's personal resources that are carried to any situation have a direct bearing upon the manner in which that situation is perceived. Jeff's and Linda's perceptions were heavily influenced by their own lack of skills. Steve, however, seemed to be energized by his personal resources as they related to that particular set of circumstances. Figure 5 shows how our personal resources influence our perceptions.

A Word of Caution

Historically, in attempting to understand and comprehend new information, concepts and ideas, we break down and dissect those ideas into segments. Oftentimes, in our quest for this increased understanding, we strive for a searching analysis by laying bare the parts of pieces for individual scrutiny. We hope by distinguishing the component parts that we will discover its true nature or inner substance and find "real" meaning. Oftentimes that ends up being counter-productive. Through emphasizing individual parts, our "analysis" can lead us down the wrong path. We can lose sight of what we were after in the first place—a striving for greater insight and understanding. The danger in all this is when we slice up the total package into smaller particles and then we look upon those particles as entities in themselves.

If that were to occur as we consider the factors that influence our perceptual experiences, the very intent and purpose would be obscured. And that would blur any increased understanding that we are seeking. To maintain proper perspective, we should approach the characteristics that influence our perceptions as sources of influence that actually exist, but are bound together in unique and individual ways in each of us. And while it is true that one facet may be in the forefront and other influences are relegated to the background, there is another important quality. Again, consider Figure 2 on page 17.

27

FIGURE 5

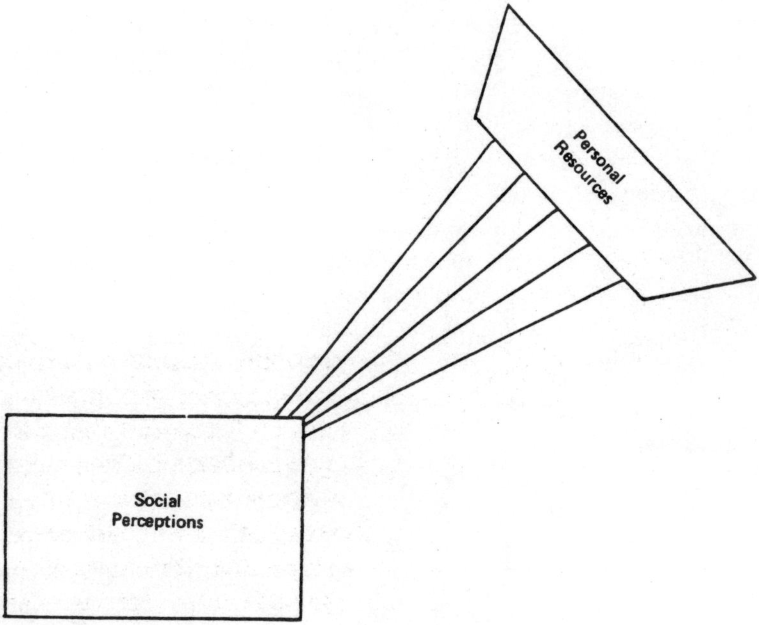

Personal Resources

Social Perceptions

That tells us that one aspect may represent our perceptual figure but oftentimes our "ground" contributes to our perceptual field and influences us in all sorts of strange ways. Figure 6 shows how our perception is influenced by all three characteristics.

It is also true that, even as we think of all of the influencing factors as having an impact, the circumstances may dictate which factor is "figure" or "ground."

* * * * * * * * * *

Brent was taking a very important exam that morning. He had studied hard and was well-prepared for the test. But that morning his alarm didn't go off. He woke up fifteen minutes before school was to start. His exam was first period. Usually it took him twenty minutes to get to school from his house. Even though he skipped dinner the night before, Brent had to do without breakfast. He was famished. He ran all the way to school and barely arrived on time. Although he took a long drink of water to fill some of the emptiness he felt, throughout the exam he had difficulty concentrating on the questions.

* * * * * * * * * *

Although Brent may experience an alternating, shifting "figure" and "ground" on many days, today was worse than usual. His intense hunger was preventing him from having enough degrees of freedom to fully attend to the task. Figure 7 shows this intensity.

* * * * * * * * * *

Tricia had many things about herself that she wished she could change. She wasn't popular. Boys never asked her out. Tricia always felt that if she had been born with the looks and the brains of her younger sister, she would have been better off. She knew her sister was better looking and was smarter. These feelings were fueled by the report cards and even by the ring of the telephone. Boys *and* girls were always calling for her sister, never her. Already her sister, who was two years younger, had more dates than Tricia ever had. Her sister had everything— grades, looks and friends.

* * * * * * * * * *

Tricia's predicament points out very clearly the manner in which the external environment such as telephone calls from friends, personal resources such as the ability to do schoolwork,

FIGURE 6

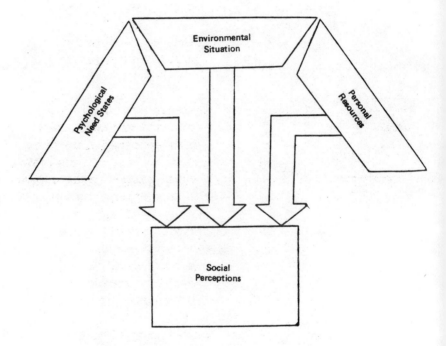

FIGURE 7

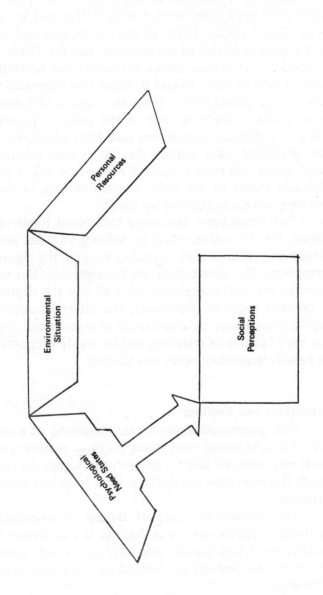

and psychological need states such as self-concept are delicately interwoven. It is true that at any given moment her perceptual figure may have been more heavily influenced by any of the three. Undoubtedly, as we all do, she experienced fluctuations in the various phases of perceptions. But for Tricia, they were all powerful generative forces in molding her perception at any given instant in time. Figure 8 shows this interrelationship and how, at any given point in time, any portion of these influences could shove everything else to the *ground*. Figure 8 shows Tricia's perceptual experiences just after her sister had gotten five telephone calls within the last fifteen minutes—and, as usual, Tricia had none. Figure 8 shows how she is preoccupied with one aspect of the external environment, or the fact that someone was always calling her sister.

But those same telephone calls could trigger another response. The net result would be feelings of stress and a loss of self-esteem. That would probably occupy the figure of one's perception. The possibilities are innumerable. But we must be aware of the frail complexity of it all and the degree that it is all blended together. Obviously, the interrelationship depends upon a precariously balanced set of characteristics. Even though that set of characteristics may not be evenly proportioned, they are heavily dependent upon one another.

Perceptions and Feelings

Our perceptual experiences, consisting of a unique mixture of psychological need states, personal resources and the external environment exert a powerful influence on our feelings. Figure 9 shows how our feelings flow from our perceptual experiences.

Our perceptual figure of the set of circumstances that eventually impacts upon our feelings is not always that clear. Usually, the figure-ground relationship is much more dynamic than that. Our feelings are formed by more than one set of circumstances.

* * * * * * * * * *

Nancy's husband promised to fix breakfast for himself and their two sons while she was gone. The morning after Nancy had left, her husband got off to a bad start. He was

FIGURE 8

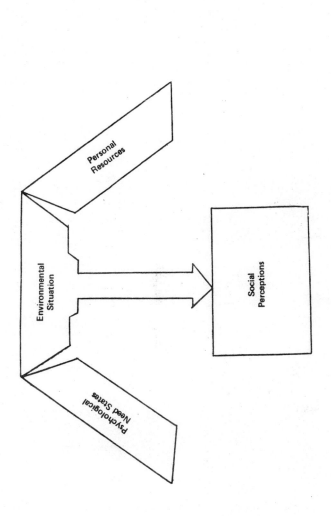

FIGURE 9

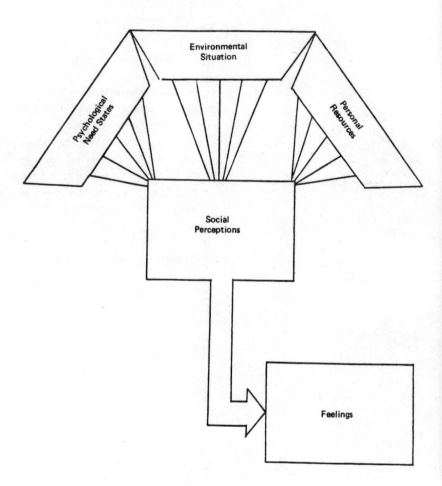

running a little late and, feeling a little hungry himself, found their two children reluctant to get out of bed and get ready for school. He went to the cupboard to get the cereal and filled the three bowls but he found no milk in the refrigerator. After experiencing momentary irritation over the environmental situation (no milk), he was able to find bread to put in the toaster and fresh fruit to eat for breakfast. Along with the instant breakfast drink, the make-shift breakfast was quite acceptable.

*   *   *   *   *   *   *   *   *   *

Many other husbands might have had a different reaction but Nancy's husband did not have a problem with self-esteem. It was not easily threatened by the environmental situation (finding no milk) or by his lack of personal resources (What do I do about breakfast?). Accordingly, he was able to respond to the environment as it actually existed. Without much effort, he mobilized his personal resources (finding another breakfast) to solve the problem he encountered.

Sounds easy. But that response might have been much different if, somewhere in that process, his self-esteem would have been threatened. If, for example, a loss of self-esteem would have been activated by not having been "properly served" by his wife, then it is probable that his primary response would have been a wounded sense of loss. Never mind that the diminished self-worth had little to do with the original issue. If his self-esteem were so fragile that finding no milk became an expression of intention to inflict damage, then the "milk" would have eased into the background and the perceptual figure would have been his sense of lost self-esteem.

That's when stress occurs, if it's going to at all. Once the light that shines overhead becomes dark with these hidden agendas, little else matters. Everything else is relegated into the foreground. Many people react to that darkened cloud by attempting to push others into that same taint of despair. Several symptoms could appear—child abuse, spouse abuse, alcoholism, drug abuse, discipline problems, delinquency, sexual promiscuity, or school attendance problems. A whole host of very real, sometimes tragic, human problems can be set in motion when these emotional responses take place.

On the other hand, a great many situations similar to the "milk" incident take place every day—and there is no stress

35

involved whatsoever. Simply put, everyday events do not trigger these stress responses in most of us—most of the time. Our self-esteem is not infringed upon that easily. Environmental situations do not usually penetrate and threaten our social perceptions in most instances because our self-esteem is "in balance" with our personal resources and the environment as it exists. Imbalance occurs when one of the three sets of circumstances weighs more heavily on our perceptions than others. Depending on the set of circumstances, if this imbalance becomes progressive, then stress may take place. When the set of circumstances are spread evenly, and are kept in proportion, a state of mental health exists.

By now it should be obvious that the set of circumstances which affects our perceptions are delicately interwoven in a very unique, individualized way. The net result is the manner in which a human being understands the social world. Thus, our perceptual experiences may be quite complicated. Or, in other circumstances, our perceptions of situations may be clear and unambiguous.

Our emotional responses, like those of our perceptual experiences, may be quite intricate and difficult to understand or they could be an obvious response to a readily observable situation. Some of our feelings that we all experience on a day-to-day basis are rejection, fear, personal loss, jealousy, helplessness, shame, embarrassment, sexual attraction and anger.

Rejection. Mr. and Mrs. Roth and their twelve-year-old daughter, Carol, were new to the neighborhood. They had moved from a small community where they had many close friends. They were anxious to meet new acquaintances. They were especially eager to have their daughter make friends with Betty across the street, who was the same age.

Mrs. Roth and Carol were invited by Betty and her mother over "for a coke." They were delighted to accept the invitation, not knowing that only a few minutes prior to their arrival their neighbor's dog had gotten loose in the house and made a shambles of many of their valued household items. As Mrs. Roth and Carol entered the house, all they felt was resentment. They were not aware that it was directed toward the dog and that it was mixed with embarrassment over what had happened. Although Betty and her mother tried to hide their

36

feelings and pretend as if there were nothing wrong, they sensed that there was definitely something wrong and that the concealed resentment was, for some reason, directed at them. After a short visit, and on the way back across the street, Mrs. Roth told Carol, "I don't think you'd better go back over there anymore."

Everyone needs acceptance. It is a vital link to our own self-esteem. If this need is denied, we feel rejected. Rejection is a very painful experience; it leads to further feelings of isolation and alienation. Usually, if we perceive that someone is rejecting us, we retaliate by rejecting that person in turn.

In order for relationships to survive, then, it would seem that we must continually communicate acceptance. Yet this is impossible. Often, in dealing with people, our own psychological needs occupy the "figure" of our perceptual experience and our social interaction is relegated to the background. Thus, no one can feel loving and accepting all the time. Psychologically, it is impossible. Then, what is the answer? How can we prevent people from perceiving that we reject them? The answer is simple, yet hard to follow. It is to say, "You are not responsible for my particular psychological state. Yet, I am disappointed over what is happening to me. *That* is what I am responding to — not you."

It is also to say that any truly effective social interaction requires at least one person setting aside his or her own needs into the background and focusing on the other person as the perceptual figure. Mrs. Roth could have said, "Looks like you had a rough time. What's wrong?" or, "You seem upset; what happened?" Instead, both were responding to their own needs and were unable to develop enough degrees of freedom to focus on the other person. And rather than a meaningful relationship developing, they ended up experiencing another perceptual figure, that of increased rejection and, for Mrs. Roth and her daughter, isolation. What a shame!

Fear. At a state fair with their three-year-old daughter, Mr. and Mrs. Walters suddenly find that little Sally is missing. Frantically they search the crowd but they do not see her anywhere. Each of them remembers reading in the morning newspaper about a kidnaping at the fair the previous day, and a cold lump of fear begins to swell up inside. Then, Mrs. Walters spots

Sally nonchalantly playing with some toys at a nearby booth.

Everyone experiences fear at some time or another. It is usually attached to some specific event. Depending on the intensity of our perceptual experience, other psychological states and external events will be immediately transferred into the background.

Personal Loss. Greg's father was always very active and concerned in his affection for Greg. He took Greg to baseball and football games, went fishing, and even played "cowboys and Indians" with him. Many of the neighborhood children came over to play at Greg's because they all enjoyed the games that his father played with them. Greg enjoyed this too, and it helped his popularity at school. One night, without warning, the dad was called out of town on an emergency regarding his business. He had no time to explain it to Greg that he was going and had no idea how long it would take. During the month that he was gone, Greg's grades began to drop and the neighborhood kids stopped coming to his house.

* * * * * * * * * *

As far as Jerry knew, his parents got along well but he hardly had time to notice for he was very busy at school with many extracurricular activities and was also active in scouting and other things that took up a good deal of time. He never saw his parents fight or argue but he rarely saw them say anything to each other at all. Then one day they told him that they were going to get a divorce, and Jerry's father moved out of the house. Jerry began doing very poorly at school and became a "behavior problem."

In both these cases, the perceived withdrawal of interest and affection on the part of the boys' parents disrupted the third level of need on Maslow's hierarchy—love and affection. The same would have resulted, with less intensity, from a perception of withdrawal on the part of anyone who was significant in their lives—a favorite teacher or close friend. The lack of intensity if these others were involved would probably involve the realm of disrupting self-esteem rather than love needs. Thus, the less intensity. But in either situation, the withdrawal would interfere with social and academic functioning. Any change in important social relationships may be perceived as a withdrawal of love or acceptance. These perceptual experiences can cause lowering of the love or self-esteem needs and could lead to ineffective functioning. The figure of the perceptual experience will focus on the loss and not on what is being encountered. We may see the students daydreaming and not concentrating.

Jealousy. Darrell had long been acclaimed as the best basketball player in his class, probably in the whole school. Then one day a new boy transferred to his class. Soon everyone was talking about how good the new boy was. Everyone was talking about how he was the best player in the city. Darrell began to act irritable with his classmates, teammates, and friends. At first, his grades remained high but his playing had suffered as he had been hogging the ball lately in practice. In spite of the new player, the team lost its next two games.

*   *   *   *   *   *   *   *   *   *

Meg was a fifth grader in a small class. There were only five girls in the whole class and they were all good friends. They even had a club called the "Fivettes" and all the girls were members. A new girl transferred into the class. Meg told the others, "If you let her join our club, I'll quit."

We feel jealous in two types of situations. One is when we want something and don't have it, and someone else does. The other is when we do have it but not as much or as good a quality as we want. Some of the common qualities which give rise to jealousy are wealth, popularity, good looks, strength, intelligence and prestige. Jealousy involves a perceived loss of self-esteem related to the perceptual figure of what others possess. Actually, the perceptual experience has a tertiary focus: (1) the characteristics which we desire that someone else has, (2) our own absence of those qualities which together form (3) a comparison of ourselves and others which lowers our self-esteem.

Helplessness. Norm went to school as usual. He discovered that his parents were having a "surprise" birthday party for him that evening. But he was a conscientious student who went to school with "work" on his mind. At school, he found that he would have four exams the next day that could be influential in his obtaining a scholarship the following year. He also learned that an additional tennis practice would be held that evening to get ready for the tournament that weekend. To top it off, his parents asked him to fix dinner for himself and his younger sister. They told Norm that they had to work late, but were really arranging for the party.

* * * * * * * * * *

Mrs. Cheney had a very tight schedule that evening. She had to be through with her grocery shopping by 4:45 in order to be home by 5:15 to start dinner. Dinner should then have been ready by 6:30 so the family could eat and she could stack the dishes before getting ready to attend the League of Women Voters meeting at which we was presiding. The line was longer in the supermarket than she expected and she was not out until 5:05. She tried to drive a little faster than usual but the rush hour traffic was jammed and the usual 30 minute drive took 45 minutes. She began to put the food away and discovered she forgot the meat she wanted to fix for dinner. At that moment, her daughter ran into the house. She was crying and was very upset. Before she could learn what was wrong with her daughter, the telephone rang. It was her husband asking, "Would it be alright if we have dinner at 7:30? I have to work late."

A sense of helplessness arises from the perception that environmental forces are too great to handle. There are insufficient resources to cope with those demands. Sometimes the demands are so great that they go beyond the realistic personal resources of anyone. The demands are too great. Other times, the person simply perceives the situation as being too great for his skill level. The perceptual figure may be one's own personal inadequacy or the perceptual experience may focus on the demands themselves. Only when the person considers alternate ways of handling the situation can the imbalance be restored. Mrs. Cheney could skip the meeting. Norm could do his best on the exams and study harder for later tests. Or he could talk to his teachers and explain the situation.

Shame. Gilbert was late for school the second time this week. Both times it happened, his parents' alarm clock had failed to go off and they were also late for work. Gilbert always liked to be early when he went places and it made him feel uncomfortable to walk into class late. As he entered the room, his teacher said, "Well, well, if it isn't Gilbert. The way you're starting this day off, I can see we're in for trouble. Even my three-year-old nephew knows enough to be on time. Do you have anything to say for yourself, young man? Well, do you?"

40

Gilbert was already feeling embarrased when he entered the room late. His perceptual figure was his own sense of discomfort as he entered the room. The added environmental burden of the teacher's statement intensified that discomfort to the point he felt ashamed. For Gilbert, the consequence of the teacher's statements led to a self-fulfilled prophecy—he had unusual difficulty concentrating on school work. As the teacher predicted, that day Gilbert tried unusual ways of acting in a feeble attempt to regain his perceived loss of self-esteem. Self-actualizing schoolwork was far removed from Gilbert's frame of reference.

Embarrassment. The baseball teams were evenly divided. Each team was one player short. And you would never know it was "only" a neighborhood sandlot game. Each team wanted to win. Although Ricky was team captain, he played badly. He had made two errors which allowed the other team to tie the game. In the last inning, Ricky was batting with two outs. He wanted to get a base hit to save a little face. Instead, he struck out by missing a high inside ball that would have walked him if he hadn't swung. At school the following day, the teachers noticed that he didn't interact well with other students.

Disappointment. Mary had been hoping to get a scholarship so that she could attend the state university next fall. In order to assure the scholarship, she had to do exceptionally well on the standard achievement test required of all applicants for the scholarship, which was administered by the school. When she met with the admissions counselor, Mary was informed that her scores fell short of the criteria set by the university.

All of us set certain standards or goals that we hope to achieve. When we fall short of these standards or goals, we experience disappointment. If we "fall short" and the dimension of social pressure is added, such as when Ricky struck out in front of his teammates, embarrassment may also be felt. Depending on certain social dynamics and emotional factors, any emotion may be experienced in combination with other feelings.

Sexual Attraction. At a very early age, even in kindergarten, children feel attracted to members of the opposite sex. Most assuredly this is not the same phenomenon that exists in adolescents or adults; it is, however, just as real. Adults —

41

parents and teachers — have a tendency to shrug it off. The children's feelings may be ignored or teased. Children who openly want to be girlfriends or boyfriends with members of the opposite sex are often teased by their peers or "kidded" by adults. Thus, from both adults and peers the child learns that there's something about interpersonal relationships with members of the opposite sex that isn't "right." He finds himself with a natural and healthy affection which he seeks to express. But in a not so subtle manner, this is often "put down."

This makes it very difficult for the child to relate to members of the opposite sex as equals. Instead, he learns to become anxious about his own natural feelings, embarrassed by them, ashamed of them. In the early elementary years, children can cope with this fairly effectively; it does not cause them much trouble to deny their relatively immature attachment. Liking a member of the opposite sex soon becomes a "secret" that will be revealed only "if you promise not to tell."

As the child emerges into adolescence, no matter how gradually, at some magical point effective peer relations with members of the opposite sex are expected. Yet, for years a general anxiety about heterosexual relationships has been felt. This anxiety is usually greater for boys because, for some reason, they are more openly "teased" by other children. It is as though we expect adolescents, as they mature, to forget their early learnings. It just doesn't happen.

Anger. Bill was a mediocre basketball player. His skills were inconsistent. When his buddies got together for a friendly game, he usually tried very hard. At times everything he shot went in the basket. During these times, even his passes seemed sharper as well. Other times, everything he tried went amiss. Bill was sensitive to his basketball skills. And, in this group, peer status had always been defined by basketball ability. One way of defining that ability was the order in which they were chosen on the teams. Because of Bill's inconsistency, he was especially sensitive to when he was chosen. That afternoon Bill watched as, one-by-one, he was passed over as the captains chose sides. Finally, when no one else was available, Bill was chosen. Bill felt anger swell up inside. He was angry at his own basketball ability, at the captains for chosing him last and his self-esteem was demolished.

42

Depending on the situation, many feelings are like those that Bill experienced. They flow from a combination of the person's psychological need states, the environmental situation and the person's resources to cope with the environment. Other feelings arise out of a dynamic blend of the set of characteristics coming together in one form or another.

Behavior

Behavior, as we all know, is influenced by feelings. Figure 10 depicts the manner in which behavior is the cumulative effect of our feelings, perceptions and set of circumstances that affects our perceptions.

Suppose you are vacationing in Colorado. As you are walking aimlessly to your cabin, you seem to be drifting; you feel no need to accomplish anything special. Suddenly you see a bear. Everything changes. Your sense of security and safety is disrupted. Your first reaction is that your perception is heightened. You experience an immediate increase in your awareness of the environmental situation—in this case a bear—which disrupts your psychological states—in this case a fear over personal safety. You also experience an increased awareness of your personal resources. You become goal oriented. Your whole body is affected. Your heart pounds. Your muscles get tight. Your intellect is called into play. You ask, "What do I know about bears? How fast can they run? How fast can I run? Can I climb that tree? Can bears climb trees?" Your whole body becomes goal oriented, unlike the aimless drifting you experienced only seconds before when none of your life forces seemed to be threatened.

But if you were in your automobile driving down a mountain road and saw the same bear, your reactions would be different. The personal resources—in this case the automobile— that you had at your disposal to cope with the environment that threatened your psychological state would be the difference.

Unfortunately, in day-to-day situations the "threat" may not be quite so visible as the bear. In fact, because the most common "threat" involves the loss of self-esteem, the environmental situation that contributes to that state may be imper-

FIGURE 10

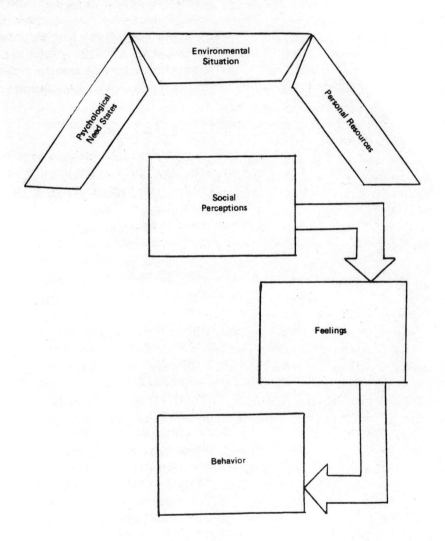

ceptible to most observers. Again, the complex union that exists among the set of circumstances to affect all this is almost inexhaustible. The important point is to become sensitive to the dynamics and aware of some of the possibilities. We, as educators, often see behavior that is difficult to understand. Hopefully, these insights can pave the way for more effective methods of dealing with students and the various problems they encounter.

Essentially, there are three general types of reactions in which people can respond during stressful conditions, regardless of which set of circumstances may be contributing to the person's perception. Those behavioral reactions are blaming, ignoring and surrendering.

Blaming. Blaming arises from any one of several, or several combinations of feelings, including anger. Generally, someone who blames other people, throws his weight around, and makes other people feel uncomfortable. The underlying message is, *"It's your fault for the way that I feel."*

     *   *   *   *   *   *   *   *   *

As Carol was taking the test, she grew increasingly uncomfortable. She wasn't all that sure she understood the questions. She simply was doing poorly. And she knew it. As she looked around, she noticed that the other students appeared relaxed and confident. This bothered Carol. Her anxiety increased. She felt that somehow others were noticing her discomfort and her own poor performance. It occurred to Carol that maybe her instructor had covered the material on the day that she missed school. As she thought about it, she felt that that must be what went wrong. As she wondered why the instructor hadn't explained the material to her the next day, she felt her face become red. She was mad. But she also felt embarrassed, and extremely disappointed, and she felt a host of other emotions she couldn't begin to identify.

When Carol walked home from school, she refused to talk to her friends. After one girl asked Carol what was wrong, Carol became upset with the girl. Carol accused the girl of wanting her to do badly on the test and *that* was the reason no one explained the material she thought she had missed.

Surrendering. Among many animals there is a way of handling an attack by another of the same species—the threatened animal lies down on the ground and exposes his throat. It is a sign of surrendering. The person who deals with any of the set of circumstances that affects one's perceptions by surrendering is dealing with stress in the same manner. The underlying message of this reaction is, *"It's my fault for the way you feel."*

* * * * * * * * * *

Julie, a fifth grader, was the younger of two sisters. She was only a year and a half younger than her older sister and, out of necessity, she usually had to wear "hand-me-downs." She never knew any other way but to be second. Patsy, her older sister, was also brighter and always brought home straight A's. As much as she tried, Julie could not compete successfully with her sister. Although Julie's parents tried not to show favoritism, it was difficult. Sibling rivalry was never very intense because Julie accepted her subordinate position.

There was one dress which both girls liked to wear to parties, and since they usually went different ways, it was ordinarily no problem. But now they had been invited to the same affair, the birthday party of a girl who knew them both. Julie wanted to wear the dress but as they were getting ready, she watched Patsy reach for the dress. Julie simply hung her head but said nothing. At the party, several people noticed that Julie wasn't having a good time. They didn't realize that her perceptual figure involved her wishing that she would have been able to wear the dress.

* * * * * * * * * *

Ignoring. Sometimes, regardless of which feelings are being experienced, the person may simply ignore and sidestep those emotions. The person may be feeling intense emotions inside. In spite of what the emotions are, there will be no outward expression toward the source of our stress. Our behavior would indicate the set of circumstances that we are really responding to, at least on the inside, is being ignored. We do not attack, or blame; nor do we give in, or submit. We simply ignore. Although we may, or may not, have strong feelings that are still attached to the "original" source, we seemingly redirect our attention to something else.

* * * * * * * * * *

Billy Joe and his brother, Allan, loved their parents very much. Partially because of everything the family did, Billy Joe

46

and Allan enjoyed increased popularity at school. The parents took their sons and their friends bowling, to ballgames and were always enjoyable for other kids to be around.

One evening at the dinner table, Billy Joe and Allan saw their parents have an argument. They were shouting at each other over some trivial incident. As the parents continued to argue, the two brothers left the dinner table. Billy Joe went outside to play with the dog. He actually forgot about the argument and had fun romping around with his favorite pet. Allan went to the basement to watch television. Although the T.V. was on and the programs were among his favorites, all he could envision was the unrealistic fear of his parents splitting up over an argument. Television was on. It looked like he was watching it, but his mind was very much on the argument taking place between his parents. His feelings were tied directly to the fear that he created about his parents separating.

*　*　*　*　*　*　*　*　*　*

A Word On Behavior

As we observe behavior in the classroom, in the lunch-room, on the playground, and in the hallways, we often observe behavior that is difficult to understand. That is because we are trying to understand what we see in relation with the external environment. We assume that a student's behavior is in response to the environment. Actually, that is often not the case. In fact, the perceptual figure of the students may not have anything to do with the environmental situation that we are able to observe. The behavior that is difficult to understand oftentimes is a response to some unmet psychological need, such as self-esteem, and not the environment, or even the pure ability to cope with that situation. Since the development of our student's self-esteem has been left to chance, it should be of little surprise that the lack of self-esteem is a major problem in our schools. As educators, we observe those dynamics on a daily basis. Therein lies the answer to one of the paradoxes we see in adolescents. That is, many are traditionally rebellious to adult authority. Yet, within their own circles, they tend to be fiercely conformist. Both sets of attitudes and behaviors flow from a struggle for self-esteem. In Maslow's framework, it is quite likely that that struggle would not be nearly as intense if self-esteem were better developed.

Another aspect of behavior that we need to consider before we begin dealing with some techniques on increasing our student's self-esteem *and* on implementing emotional education is to recognize that behavior results in certain consequences. There is an inter-personal consequence attached to every behavior we engage in. Figure 11 integrates the concept of consequences as it relates to the approach.

Thus, our perception of a situation leads to feelings that leads to behavior that results in certain interpersonal consequences. This is not a suggestion of behavioral determinism; rather, it is used as a tool to understand the behavior that we see. The concept of behavioral alternatives is an integral part of the model. That is, there is more than one way to handle the same feeling. While those behavioral patterns would be quite variable among people, some approaches are more effective than others. The effectiveness of our social behaviors is related to the interpersonal consequences that we seek.

FIGURE 11

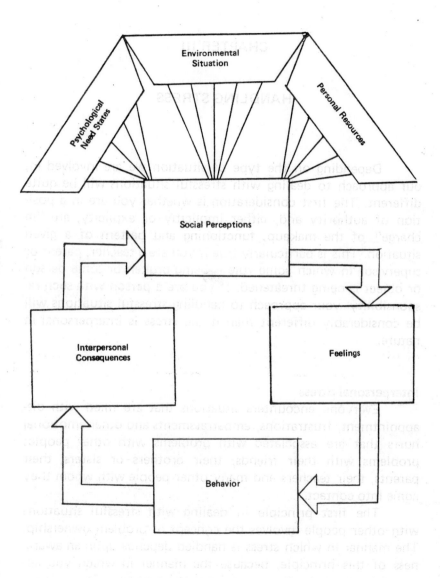

CHAPTER III

HANDLING STRESS

Depending on the type of situation we are involved in, our approach to dealing with stressful situations will be quite different. The first consideration is whether you are in a position of authority and, either implicitly or explicity, are "in charge" of the makeup, functioning and pattern of a given situation. This is particularly true if you are a teacher, parent or supervisor in which some rule is being broken or some person or object is being threatened. If you are a person with such responsibility, your approach to handling stressful situations will be considerably different than if the stress is interpersonal in nature.

Interpersonal Stress

Everyone encounters situations that are filled with disappointment, frustrations, embarrassments and other emotional hurts that are associated with problems with other people: problems with their friends, their brothers or sisters, their parents, their teachers and many other people with whom they come into contact.

The first principle in dealing with stressful situations with other people involves the concept of problem ownership. The manner in which stress is handled depends upon an awareness of this principle, because the manner in which you approach stress depends on who owns the problem. This is intuitively obvious. You would behave in a different manner if you were feeling stressful than you would if your friend were feeling some underlying stress.

If your friend owned the problem, you would want to come across in a sensitive, understanding manner. The other person owns a problem when he or she is thwarted in satisfying a need, when the personal resources are woefully inadequate, or if there is something occurring in the external environment that is threatening. You own the problem if you have some feeling that needs to be expressed about what the other person is doing or about some other aspect about the immediate social environment that is upsetting.

If the other person owns the problem, or is experiencing stress, and if that person decides to communicate with you, or another person, that is happening because he or she has a need. It is because there is something going on inside. That person owns the problem and is experiencing stress because some discomfort is being felt and he or she is upset about something or there is some emotional pain. Usually, the stress is, in some form, coming from one of the three sources of influence that affects a person's perception of himself interacting within a given situation. If, on the other hand, you were experiencing stress and you owned the problem, your feelings would be similarly affected.

Because the ways of handling stress are quite dependent upon where the source of stress lies, the chart on the following page may be helpful in showing the difference between the roles when the ownership of the problem changes.

Listening to another person when he or she is experiencing stress or, in some other way owns a problem takes a lot of energy, active involvement, and an ability and willingness to give the other person center stage. That is easier said than done. The other person, as a living, feeling human being, is what you, as a listener, are actively concentrating upon. Active listening is not a natural talent. It is a skill that needs to be learned and practiced.

Actually, in order to grasp the sad state of affairs that some of our listening skills are in, all you have to do is be aware of some of the conversations taking place on a routine basis. Many of our "conversations" involve no interchange whatsoever. Let's take a look at a typical coffee room conversation. This is an example of parallel listening. Person A begins talking.

When you own the problem:	When the other person owns the problem:
You are more aggressive	You are a listener
You are more interested in your needs.	You try to help the other person understand his feelings.
You are the "sender" of communication.	You are the "receiver" of communication
You want to sound off.	You are the sounding board
You want, and need, someone to really listen to how you feel	Someone else needs to be listened to—and that is your role
Your feelings and needs represent your perceptual figure	Requires an effort on your part to accept the other person's problem *and* a willingness to place your needs and wants into the back*ground*. The other person's need for communication must be allowed "in" to your perceptual figure.

Person A's statement:	I like the blue dress.	Maybe I'll buy it.	My husband wouldn't mind. He likes blue.
Person B's response:	The brown one is pretty.	The brown one isn't very expen- sive.	But I already have a brown dress.

What happened? Person A started the conversation by making a simple statement. Really what was happening were two separate, parallel, one-side conversations. This is called "parallel" listening because of the one-sided nature of what is being said. Never will their paths cross. After such an encounter, both will go away without a sense of having been listened to. Both were relegating each other to the back*ground* of each other's perceptual field. Both were unwilling to "give." Such a conversation could have gone on and on with no one ever listening to the other.

There are two main types of listening. *Conversational listening* involves the give and take that takes place when there is no interpersonal stress. In *conversational listening*, the skill required is to focus upon the *behavior* of the other person, or what has been said. *Active listening* may be beneficial when there is some felt stress on the part of the sender. The listener does not focus on the *behavior*, or what was said; rather, the receiver is much more active than that. The other person's feelings and possible perceptual experiences must be the "figure" of the listener.

Conversational Listening

Conversational listening is differentiated from active listening because it does not run as "deep" as active listening. Active listening goes beyond the behavior, or what has been said, while conversational listening gives prominence to the verbal behavior. Let's take the previous example on parallel listening.

Person A's statement:	I like the blue dress	No, he hasn't seen it. Maybe I'll buy it.	Not usually, but he likes blue.
Person B's response:	Really. Does your husband like it too?	Wow. Would you really buy it before he saw it?	

This is only an example of the *kind* of responses that are involved in conversational listening. Person B could have made any of a number of statements that would have been in *response to what Person A said*. But notice the difference between the two examples of parallel listening and conversational listening. Conversational listening, while not as deep as active listening, still involves an ability and willingness to place the other person and what is being said into the figure of your perception. It can also mean that each person is able to introduce some conversation into the verbal exchange. This type of give and take is essential for spontaneous talking and listening.

Active Listening

Active listening is a useful communication tool when the other person owns the problem, or some type of stress is being experienced. Active listening goes beyond what the other person says, or the behavior. What is going on inside the other person is the emphasis. These feelings and perceptual experiences are, in some manner, creating a problem—or stress— for the other person. The listener is actively involved in trying to *understand and clarify* the perceptions and feelings of the other person. When this takes place with a person who is feeling stress, at least two phenomena occur. First of all, the distressed person's perception is altered. In other words, there is the awareness that another person really cares about "me and my problems." And that perception by itself may relieve some personal stress. As the awareness grows that the listener is actively involved to a meaningful extent in the perceptions and feelings, the perceptual experience of the person often begins to include the listener as a caring person. As this new perception emerges into the "figure," the old stressful problem may fade into the background. Of course, the extent to which this happens depends upon a variety of circumstances, but the phenomenological properties do, to some degree, take place.

Active listening is more than a technique. It also involves a set of attitudes about the relationship with the other person. Active listening is a method for putting to work this set of attitudes. Without a proper set of attitudes, the active listening may be perceived as phony and mechanical. If the given set of attitudes do exist, active listening may be extremely useful in helping another person when he or she is experiencing stress. Here is a list of attitudes that will be helpful in active listening:

1. You must want to hear what the other person has to say about underlying feelings and perceptions.
2. This means that YOUR perceptual figure would be the other person and his feelings and perceptions that may have contributed to the stress.
3. This also means that you have no hidden agendas. You must be willing and able to shove your needs, feelings and wants to the background.
4. You must be able to genuinely accept the feelings of the other person, whatever they may be, or however different they may be from your own feelings or from the feelings you think that person SHOULD feel.
5. You must trust how they feel about the situation they perceive themselves to be in.
6. Any clarification or attempts to amend what is being said should *concentrate on their perceptions —not the feelings about the perceptions*. Statements such as:

    "Gee, I don't blame you for feeling bad. That is rough. But when I saw that happen I didn't think she was laughing at you. The way I saw it was different. I thought Julie was relieved that the test was over."

7. Understand that active listening does not have to be long and drawn out. It can be a brief encounter that may need only a few exchanges.

Here are two examples in which active listening is used in a stressful situation and in which conversational listening is used in the same situation. Notice the manner in which active listening emphasizes the feelings and perceptions while the conversational listening responds more to the behavior, or what was said.

* * * * * * * * * *

Paul was walking home alone after school. He had just gotten back a test in which he was hoping to get an A. He learned that he had passed the exam but barely received a passing grade. He felt a combination of disappointment at his own performance, irritation at his teacher for asking such irrelevant questions, and jealousy over his friend, Jeff, having done so well on the exam. He walked home alone because he didn't want to be that close to Jeff and his other friends.

Let's see what happened when Paul walked inside and his mother was listening at the conversational level, or listening to the behavior:

Paul: (Walking into the house with a frown on his face and slamming the door with a loud bang.)

Mother: Paul, don't slam the door. Go back outside and come back in. This time close it the right way.

Paul: (Stomps outside. Things feel worse than they did when he walked in. Paul walks back inside in a defiant manner, but he shuts the door the "right" way. He goes to his room and, all by himself, cries.)

Paul's mother "listened" to Paul's *behavior* and did not attempt to go "deeper" than that. His behavior, not his feelings, was what she saw, and her response was based upon that superficial approach.

Let's see what might have happened if his mother actively listened to Paul's feelings:

Paul: (Walking into the house with a frown on his face and slamming the door with a loud bang.)

Mother: Hi Paul, what's wrong? Looks like things didn't go well today. You had a rough day, huh?

Paul: (Still saying nothing, but he goes to the family room, still feeling badly.)

Mother: Things are pretty rough. I'd like to hear about it.

Paul: I didn't get an A on that test.

56

Mother: Really. I'm sorry about that. You were really looking forward to doing well, too. You must be awfully disappointed.

Paul: Yeah. And everything I knew she didn't even ask. I couldn't believe some of those stupid questions. I didn't even study for that stuff.

Mother: You studied for all the wrong things. Boy that *is* too bad.

Paul: Jeff got 'em right. He knew what to study for.

Mother: Hmmm. Somehow that makes it even worse, doesn't it?

Paul: You better believe it.

Mother: Tough luck. Wish I could help, son. But I just want you to know I'm still proud of you and I'm glad you are my son.

Paul: Thanks. (feeling a little better.)

No, it is true that problems won't magically melt away if active listening is used when somebody is experiencing stress. The problem that the other person has won't dissolve. But the stress can be relieved through successfully "connecting" with another person who really cares. As a listener, you link up with another person's feelings and emotions about some perceptual experience. The behavior, either verbal behavior or (as in Paul's case) some other manifestation, is short-circuited in favor of a more subjective and personal endeavor.

This all seems somewhat easy. In conversational listening, we respond to what is being said or some other non-verbal behavior such as, in Paul's case, slamming the door. In active listening, when another person is experiencing stress, we respond to underlying feelings and perceptions. But, as usual, nothing is as easy as it seems.

In fact, our perception of another person who is experiencing stress may have the net result of creating some of those same stressful feelings in ourselves. When that happens, it is easy to respond to our own stress, not the other person's. And then we don't listen to either the behavior or the underlying feelings. We may *blame, surrender* or *ignore*. Again, it is important to note that these are reactions to *our* stress—not the other person's. As an example, let's see what some of these responses might have been in Paul's situation.

57

1. Blaming (seeing and hearing Paul slam the door)
    1. "PAUL, NOW STOP IT!"
    2. "Okay, little baby, what's wrong with you THIS time?"
    3. "Now that was a dumb thing to do."
    4. "Thanks a lot, Paul. You've really done it this time."
    5. "Why did you do that?"
2. Surrendering.
   Usually, in surrendering there is no direct, verbal response to another person's feelings. But the mother may have thought to herself:
    1. "Better not say anything to Paul. He's mad."
    2. "That's not usually like Paul. He's a good boy."
    3. (Cringing) "Poor Paul. Wonder who was mean to him today?"

   Sometimes it is possible to surrender to another person's stress by blaming someone else. We must remember, however, that it really is surrendering to the person's stress.
    4. "Now what did those lousy kids do to you, Paul?"
    5. "Those rotten classmates." (implying "What did *they* do to my poor, picked-on boy).
    6. "I never did like your being around those kids anyway."
3. Ignoring.
    1. "I've felt that way myself."
    2. "You'll feel better tomorrow."
    3. "Just forget about it."
    4. "What's on T.V. tonight?"
    5. "Five more weeks and school will be out."
    6. "Remember last week when you were picked for the class play? Didn't that make you feel good?"

   In ignoring the other person's stress, we are trying not to deal with it *because of how we feel*. So we try to get the other person "away" from the problem by withdrawing from the problem ourselves and trying to take the other person with us. We use distraction; we may attempt to kid him out of it. But the essential feature is that we push the problem aside.

If You Own The Problem

Instead of blaming, surrendering or ignoring our experienced stress, we need to learn to deal with it directly and effectively. — Before these strategies are dealt with, there is a subtle distinction that needs to be made. And that distinction is directly related to whether or not a feeling of stress is involved.

At times it may be entirely appropriate to blame, ignore or surrender to a specific situation. At times, it may even be appropriate to resort to these tactics if we feel stressful. For instance, if our boss tells us to do something, and we experience stress because of what he has said, it might be beneficial for us to "surrender." Other examples could be given. We may choose to ignore sources of potential problems. That could well be the healthiest thing to do.

But these are not the issues that we are presently dealing with. We are trying to deal with stress in interpersonal situations.

Entirely different communication skills are needed when you "own" the problem as compared to when someone else is experiencing stress, or "owns" a problem. Probably the single most important issue revolves around putting the "I" involvement back into the verbal exchange, especially on the part of the sender. Oftentimes we camouflage our underlying stress by *naming someone else to describe our feelings.* Such peculiarities are, in part, consequences of the way we communicate. For example, when we name someone else to describe how *we* feel, we are actually talking more about ourselves than we are the other person. When we say "Tom is stupid," we really mean, "When I perceive Tom's inability to learn something, I feel disappointed." Or, when we say "Tom is smart," we really mean, "When I perceive Tom's ability to learn quickly, I feel proud."

One easy way to understand this is to think of these differences as "you messages" or "I messages." When we name someone else, there is always, either explicitly or implicitly, a "you message" involved in the communication. Typical "you messages" may start out with communications like these:

> "*That is* a dumb thing to do."
> "You are acting like a. . . ."
> "You are . . . ."

"Jerry is . . . ."

"Cory, that is . . . ."

When the owner of stress simply tells the other person what is being perceived and how that (behavior) is making you feel, the message usually turns out to be an "I" message.

Then, instead of naming someone else, we can hear such statements as:

"I'm awfully tired. I don't feel like playing now."

"Looks to me like I didn't get invited. I sure felt left out."

"It's getting late and dinner isn't even close to being ready. Sorry, but I don't feel that I have time right now."

"I was really looking forward to getting an A on that test.

You won't believe how disappointed I was. Boy, I was let down."

The "I" message is much less likely to provoke resistance and stress on the part of the listener. This is because you are talking about your feelings, about your perceptions—you are not attaching a name to someone else to describe your feelings. Also, to communicate honestly in this manner about, for example, your perception of that behavior and how you feel about it is much less threatening than to suggest there is something bad about him or her as a person.

For Parents and Teachers: Handling Stressful Situations

As parents and teachers, we are the architects of the personalities of our sons, daughters and students. We are in a very unique and unusual position. Either intentionally or by default, we have it within our sphere of command to mold and shape the emotional and social lives of these young human beings. Like it or not, to these children, you are a powerful adult who superintends the formation of their lives. Make no mistake about it. As a potential source of influence, we are much too powerful to ignore it or to act as if it doesn't really matter.

The teaching of responsibility is of crucial importance. Responsibility means the ability to satisfy one's own feelings and wants while, *at the same time*, consideration is given to the

60

interpersonal consequences of that behavior. A responsible person is able to behave in such a way that gives him a feeling of self-worth and, under appropriate conditions, self-actualization. He or she is also able to give other people a sense of self-worth. A responsible person does not create undue stress in others, and handles it well when stress is encountered.

All this sounds fine. But how does one learn to be responsible to the point that there is sensitivity to his/her feelings and needs as well as other people's feelings and needs? Not surprisingly, learning responsibility is a complicated and delicate matter. The acquisition of this sensitivity can be a natural and fun experience, but there are certain basic psychological principles that makes these learnings much easier to cultivate.

Around the turn of the century, a Russian psychologist by the name of Pavlov set forth some basic principles of learning that, for the most part, have gone largely unnoticed by modern psychologists who deal with emotions, motivations and basic social learnings of human beings. Pavlov was an experimental psychologist. As a result, he worked mostly with animals as he extracted and understood basic psychological principles from his experimental work. No attempt will be made to delve into the details of his research. An abundance of psychological literature already concerns itself with that part of Pavlov's work. What is crucial is what Pavlov learned and how those learnings can be applied to our everyday lives. He taught us the difference between a Conditioned Stimulus and an Unconditioned Stimulus. An Unconditioned Stimulus is something that requires no learning in order to appreciate and comprehend its value. Because of some intrinsic properties that the Unconditioned Stimulus holds, its value is not determined by conditioning or learning. It is of natural value. Food has an intrinsic value to us all and, therefore, would be called an Unconditioned Stimulus. Spanking. or some other physical pain, also requires no conditioning or learning for us to appreciate its meaning. Because of these natural properties, the Unconditioned Stimulus will be referred to as the Natural Stimulus.

A Conditioned Stimulus, on the other hand, has no natural, intrinsic value. A Conditioned Stimulus is something we *learn* to value *because of its association with a natural stimulus*. Money, for example, has no natural or intrinsic value. Money is valuable only because we can acquire those items which we naturally cherish, such as food, shelter, etc. The Conditioned Stimulus will be referred to as the Learned Stimulus.

Pavlov has taught us that if we pair a learned stimulus with a natural stimulus over a long period of time, the learned stimulus *will take on the same properties as the original, natural stimulus.*

This has implications in parenting and in teaching. In parenting, we can begin to understand the importance of showing the child physical *and* verbal affection when the infant is feeding. Through this type of association, the affection that the infant receives from the parent takes on new importance. The implications extend into later years as well. If a feeling statement is paired with some natural reinforcing stimulus, the child can learn sensitivity to other people's feelings. For example:

Feeling Statement (Learned Stimulus)	Natural Stimulus
"I really like it when you play that way, Johnny."	"Because I like what I see, I have brought you all popsicles."

Over a period of time, the parent's feelings begin to take on the same value as the natural stimulus, whatever that is. The child learns sensitivity to other people's feelings and learns that those feelings are important to him or her.

Now, it is also true that, during times of discipline, the same approach may be used. For example:

Feeling Statement (Learned Stimulus)	Natural Stimulus
"I don't like it when you hurt your brother by hitting him so hard."	"You must go and sit in the chair by yourself for ten minutes, or until you really know how to control that type of behavior."

The Natural Stimulus doesn't have to involve food. The need for activity is also a natural need. But, we must be careful. *We must spend more time catching the child at being good than we do at being bad.* Or else, our interaction with our child will begin to take on those negative elements, and our relationship with our child will suffer. We must remember that the most important thing we have going with our child is that relationship that we have with our son or daughter.

Actually, some of the same principles that are needed in parenting are also useful in teaching. In teaching the young people in our classrooms, it is imperative that the teacher personally relate to the child as well as set appropriate behavioral limits. Relating to the students in a warm and human manner, however, may seen inconsistent with setting the necessary limits that provide for classroom stability. In fact, it may seem as if the teacher is caught in an unenviable dilemma. But that is not an unavoidable trap. If verbal interaction with appropriate accompanying consequences are used, then the solution to the "trap" seems reasonably likely.

Interaction With Positive Consequences

Interaction with positive consequences encourages the appropriate behavior that facilitates learning. This would be behavior that is compatible with class rules and incompatible with any possible problem "target" behaviors that may be of concern. Any behavior that is incompatible with "problem" behaviors may be included here. For example, sitting quietly while studying would be incompatible with acting-out behaviors and would also facilitate learning. Particular attention should be paid to those students who typically engage in an inordinate amount of misbehavior, although no student's appropriate behavior should be taken for granted. As with the role of the parents, this simply means to "catch the child at being good."

Depending upon each child's relative rate of misbehaving, any sign of appropriate class behavior should be commented on. One effective way of doing this, while simultaneously emphasizing your *feelings* about what he is doing, is to employ the "I" message along with a statement about your perception of that behavior.

Teacher's Perception	"I" Message
"Looks to me like you are really working hard right now."	"I feel proud when you do that."

The "I" Message always involves a feeling such as, "I am proud," or "I really like that," and is associated with a description of the child's behavior as it is perceived by the teacher. This manner of "catching the child at being good" emphasizes the teacher's feelings, giving additional credence to the value of human emotion.

Although not always possible, a third element to this communication is extremely beneficial. And that would involve a positive consequence for appropriate behavior.

Teacher's Perception:	"Looks to me like you are really working hard right now."
"I" Message:	"I really feel proud when you do that."
Positive Consequence:	"Because I like what you are doing, the whole class may have five minutes extra recess."

Using this kind of feedback with positive consequences, the appropriate working behaviors may be maintained and increased by three reinforcers: (1) The immediate gratification of receiving the extra privilege; (2) Developing social reinforcement for the child's working behaviors from his peers (the classmates will become more attentive to these positive behaviors); and (3) Becoming more successful in school as a result of spending more time on a task, thereby finding schoolwork more rewarding. In addition, the teacher's feelings become more potent and powerful so that, before long, the child will begin to become sensitive to the feelings of the teacher. Over a period of time, this sensitivity to the teacher's feelings will generalize to other people's feelings. Students who experience this approach at home and in the school will be more sensitive and aware of the emotions of other people and how their behavior affects those feelings. This is not achieved at the expense of children's self-esteem. Children learn the value of their own feelings *and* to respect other people.

Interaction with Negative Consequences

There are those professionals who suggest that it is best to completely ignore students when they act up, misbehave, or in some way interfere with the learning or performance of others. They maintain that students should be given attention *only* when they behave within a set of class limits. Indeed, "catching the child at being bad" could very well exacerbate undesirable behaviors. This seems to happen for two reasons: (1) The child is given attention for misbehaving which, for him, may actually be rewarding; and (2) The typical way of "catching the child at being bad" may strengthen the already existing notion that "I am bad," or "I am a pest." The resultant interaction may be something like this:

Teacher's Perception:	Seeing Johnny running around and disrupting some of the class.
Verbal Description:	"Stop it. How many times do I have to tell you?"
Child's Perceptual Experience:	"I am a pest."

In addition to strengthening the idea that the child is "no good," this oftentimes is the child's chief way of getting attention and, although negative, he or she may actually seek out this type of feedback. Typically, no negative consequence results from this disruptive behavior, only the teacher's reprimand. Not only is this reprimand ineffective, but it may contribute to the problem because: (1) No consequence is associated with it; (2) It reinforces the "I am bad" syndrome; and (3) The student learns to ignore the teacher's feelings.

The "I" message associated with a description of the teacher's perception and a negative consequence may be just what the student needs.

Teacher's Perception:	"Johnny, looks to me like you are running around and bothering other people. That stops other kids from working and it also means you were not doing your work."
"I" Message:	"I really don't like it, and I really feel disappointed."
Negative Consequences:	"Because I don't like what I see, you will not be allowed to get a drink of water during break."

When the combination of the "I" message, description of the teacher's perception and negative consequences are used, the student's own perception is changed. Instead of thinking of himself as a pest, the child perceives something different, namely:

Student's Perception

"I can't get a drink of water for what I did. The teacher didn't like it."

Not only does this make the child less defensive than the "you stop running around" approach, but it also makes the child responsible for what he does—it removes a privilege that otherwise would have belonged to that student. Unlike positive consequences, negative consequences should *never be extended to the entire class or other classmates.* The child's misbehavior should remain totally his or her own, and only those who misbehave should be held responsible.

Some Cautions

These tools, if used over an extended time span, can be effective in classroom management *and* in maximizing the learnings about human emotions and interpersonal consequences. But it is crucial that more time should be spent catching kids at "being good" than is spent in catching them at "being bad." Otherwise, we are telling our students how not to behave but we are not replacing that with information on how to behave. We cannot afford to leave a void. Otherwise, that misbehavior could well be replaced by other misbehavior. Our effectiveness would be decreased—and the learnings would be minimized.

Also, we cannot afford for the students to perceive these methods and techniques as being attached to some "goodness" or "badness" on the part of the child. Consequences should not be associated with, "I got it because I am good," or "I didn't get something because I am bad." If so, everything you as a teacher are trying to do will be substantially reduced in value. We simply cannot afford to reduce another human being down to "goodness" or "badness" or something very precious will be lost.

CHAPTER IV

TEACHING EMOTIONAL EDUCATION
IN THE CLASSROOM

The activities and game type situations that are presented in the remainder of the book represent an attempt to sequence the material in a developmental manner. Actually, this is similar to the approach of other areas of education. That is, fundamentals are taught that provide the groundwork for later learnings. For example, in math our students must be able to count before they can add or subtract. Then they can learn multiplication, division and more abstract concepts. Also, our students must be able to recognize letters of the alphabet before they can read words. Then they are able to read sentences. In the area of "basic skills," such as reading and math, it is more possible to readily identify the developmental stages in which learning occurs than it is in other areas, such as science or history. When the subject area is human relations, it becomes even more difficult to delineate measurable stages in which learning occurs. Thus, the concepts that can be taught in the area of emotional education are not purely additive. In other words, if a fourth grade student has not been exposed to earlier material, it would be possible—even desirable— to provide systematic exposure to that student in emotional education.

As we proceed, we must be aware of at least two factors. First of all, the developmental approach to emotional education does not represent finite, concrete stages in the sense that students must "pass through" one stage before being exposed to another. It just doesn't work that way. Rather, we must view the different levels of emotional education as being more generalized and less defined. We must view the earlier stages as laying the groundwork and providing the fundamentals —making later learnings easier and more effective.

The second word of caution applies to most areas of education. That is, as educators we should all understand that there might be important variation in students' affective readiness for these activities in emotional education. Some students might be ready for these tasks; others might not. But educators have been aware for a number of years of the situation regarding individual variability in terms of reading readiness, math readiness and so on. As in other areas, this set of instructional experiences must be geared toward the level of the class. Furthermore, within any classroom, any unique situation that exists must be recognized and understood. Variability of activities in emotional education then becomes possible—even preferred.

There are some crucial advantages to presenting a set of activities in emotional education even when a student or two may not quite be ready for the activities. Those advantages have to do with the crucial impact that social modeling and peer relationships have on everyone in the class—even those who lack "readiness." As the emotional sensitivity and social interrelationships within any milieu—including the classroom—increase, then the benefits are experienced by all. And those who lack the emotional readiness are able to move along with the classmates and make as much progress as their peers. In some cases, they may even "catch up."

One last word of caution. While we can expect marked and observable improvement in the students' social functioning as a result of experiencing emotional education, we still cannot expect "perfection." There will still be problems. Only now, the students will have a tool to understand and cope with those problems more effectively. But we should not reasonably expect more out of emotional education than any other area. We understand that physical education will produce better physical fitness—not that everyone will become four-minute-milers. Or, even though our students take courses in math, we still understand that they will need to consult bankers or accountants for advice in complicated matters. Some will be more effective at applying their math skills than others. We understand this. It is

68

a courtesy that should be extended to emotional education.

A good, practical and useful activity in emotional education isn't too long. Nor does it attempt to cover too much information. These can all reduce the effectiveness of the activities. Above all, in order to be truly effective, emotional education *does not* consist only of a special course in these activities that are presented. We must practice what we teach. We must practice and extend this approach to other areas of the curriculum *and* to everyday social situations that occur on the playground, in the lunchline, during recess and in the classroom. Here are some basic ingredients of successful activities in emotional education:

First, the teacher or counselor breaks the class down into small discussion groups. The groups should consist of five to seven in a group with each group having a group leader.

The task of the group leader changes with the age of the students. At the early elementary level, the leader's task is to listen to what the members are saying **and** *to write the responses on a piece of paper. The leader does not judge or evaluate what is being said. The leader simply listens and records what is said. During the first through third grades, it is preferable to have older students, in the fifth or sixth grades, serve as leaders. At the older elementary level, the leaders may be chosen on a rotating basis within each group. This situation may vary depending upon the needs of the class.*

Interested parents may serve as discussion leaders in the place of older students or in the place of the rotating leaders at the older elementary levels. And parents may also serve as discussion leaders at the earlier levels in the place of older students.

Secondary level discussion may be held within the small group method or the discussion may be held as an entire class.

The teacher or counselor presents the situation or stimulus and most of the "work" is done in small groups. The teacher and/or counselor may want to float among the groups to serve as an advisor.

After each period of small group discussion, the final stage of the activity involves each small group reporting to the rest of the class their opinions and ideas. This usually broadens the range of ideas and options in the minds of students.

The teacher or counselor has the responsibility for the success of the activities. First of all, the activities must be in an atmosphere of openness and trust. Yet, there must be a controlled classroom climate in which some of the techniques in Chapter III are practiced. After presenting the stimulus, the teacher or counselor must listen in a supportive way to the ideas discussed by each small group.

In addition to the activities that are presented and in addition to the manner in which the teacher relates to the students, another way of integrating these principles into the regular curriculum would be to adapt some of the "Behavior Analysis" type of questions into the mainstream of the regular curriculum. This can be accomplished by asking questions about people in current events, social studies, or characters in a Reading Book.

Here are some goals for emotional education for the various grade levels, first grade through secondary levels. You are reminded to approach these curriculum activities in the same manner as other material. That is, the activities must be used in a flexible and open manner. It is quite possible, for example, that a third grade teacher may choose to use some of the material from another grade level, depending upon the needs of the class. The activities, by grade level, are guidelines. Some activities, such as "Known and Unknown Friends" and "Changing Positions" are designed to be used at various grade levels.

Grade Levels	Goals
First Grade	To begin to learn to understand one's feelings and to accept those feelings in ourselves and others. Also, first grade students can begin to learn to communicate about their feelings.

Grade Levels	Goals
Second Grade	To continue learning to accept and recognize one's feelings by increasing our vocabulary. Also, these students can begin learning that feelings can cause behavior.
Third Grade	To strengthen the concept that feelings can cause behavior. We also want to emphasize the need for self-concept and how peer relations are tied into that feeling.
Fourth Grade	Continue increasing our sensitivity toward other people's feelings while, at the same time, learning the concept of behavioral alternatives; that is, there is more than one way to handle *our* feelings. Also, we begin to teach the influence that our social perceptions have upon our feelings.
Fifth Grade	The concept of interpersonal consequences is introduced and, with it, an increased sensitivity to the manner in which social encounters are handled. Also, the basic skills of listening at the behavioral level are introduced.
Sixth grade	Should be able to understand the idea of behavioral alternatives enough to utilize these concepts in "real life" situations. Also, new skills in communication, both languaging and listening, are learned. These skills are then practiced in a variety of simulated sessions.

Secondary Level

Course I	The goals at this level include strengthening the skills learned at the earlier levels. We also want to integrate the concepts and to show the interdependence of the "parts."

	Goals

Course II   We want the students to learn the dynamics of social perceptions and the skills involved in active listening and when to use those skills.

Course III   The skills we have learned are utilized in a variety of situations that involve interpersonal stress. Students learn to handle streeful situations both in a personal manner and if they are "in authority" as a parent or teacher. The utilization of consequences as a parent or teacher is also compared to not utilizing consequences if the stress is of an interpersonal nature.

First Grade

Naming Feelings

The class is broken into small groups with each group having a group leader. The task of each group is simply to identify as many feelings as possible. Group leaders are to write down what their group identifies. At the end of this portion of the activity, group leaders report to the teacher the feelings that were identified and the teacher then writes each feeling on the chalkboard. This way the class could see and hear all feelings that had been identified. The teacher could then spend a few minutes on the list by reading each feeling and the number of times it had been identified. Then, the teacher could ask, one feeling at a time, how many students in class had ever experienced each feeling.

Homework

At the end of the first session on *Naming Feelings*, the teacher would ask each student to do a homework assignment for the following week. Each student would have as an assignment the task of identifying at least one feeling that was not identified by the class and, therefore, was not on the chalkboard. Students are then asked to work with their parents on this assignment by having a parent write down the name of the

72

feeling and what the child thinks it means. The point should be emphasized that this is not a test and that there may be many meanings for the same feeling. Each student is then asked to bring back the name of the feeling on a piece of paper and a written description of what the feeling means.

The next session would then involve each student handing his/her paper to the group's leader. The leader would then read the names of new feelings and their meanings to the rest of the class. Again, it would be more meaningful if the teacher would write the list of new feelings on the chalkboard. Once again, the teacher could ask the students if they have ever experienced any of the newly identified feelings. Students could then be given a chance to talk about what happened to cause some of these feelings. This is strictly voluntary. The teacher could ask something like this: "Does anyone remember when you felt this way? Would anyone like to share with the rest of us what happened?"

Group Dictionaries

At least five sessions will be needed for this series of activities. The goal of this game is to make a 12" x 18" picture dictionary of feelings. The teacher would assign each group several feelings to be described by their own picture dictionary. Each group should have assigned the same number of feelings there are students in the group. That way, each student would have a chance to share with the rest of the class at least one picture dictionary.

For each session, the groups will have a sheet of 12" x 18" construction paper. On one side of the construction paper there will be written the name of a feeling. The task of each group is to describe that feeling by cutting and pasting pictures from old magazines. On the side of construction paper that is opposite from the name of the feeling, students are then to find pictures from magazines that in some way show or describe the feeling that is written. Each student in the group must find at least one picture that "defines" the feeling. The teacher will keep each group's work in a "safe" place where other students do not find it accessible.

At the end of five such sessions (or whatever number that equates to the number of students in the largest group), each student will have an opportunity to go before the entire class to show the rest of the class some feeling. Remember, the rest of the class does not know which feeling is being "defined" because the written word is on the opposite side of what is visible to the class. So the rest of the class, excluding the small group that created the picture dictionary, is to guess what feeling is being shown. This is a fun series of activities that also increase our learnings.

Short Narratives

Short narratives can be easily and effectively integrated into the regular experiences of first grade students. Story hour is a commonly used teaching device. As usual, the story is introduced and read to the pupils. The main difference involves guiding the students into thinking about some of the feelings that the characters in the story were experiencing. Not only does this aid the students in understanding, recognizing and identifying feelings, but it also leads to a more effective way of thinking about behavior—a way that takes into account the meaning or causes of behavior instead of merely its superficial form. And this is also an appropriate lead into the second grade materials that deal directly with the concept of feelings causing behavior. Here are some examples of narratives and discussion questions that encourage understanding feelings.

Getting Big

Ronnie sat up in bed. This was his big day. This was his first day of school. He was excited. Absolutely thrilled. Now he could walk to school with his big brother. He really liked and admired his brother. David, his brother, was someone he had always looked up to.

Ronnie ran down to the breakfast table. His dad and David were already eating breakfast. Mom was getting the toast buttered in the kitchen. Ronnie very excitedly asked his brother, "WHAT TIME DO WE GO TO SCHOOL, DAVID? This is my big day. I can walk to school with you. Wow!"

David put down his spoon. He said, "I am walking by myself. You can't go with me. I can't have a little brother tagging along."

(Suggested stopping place for questions.)

Teacher should ask:

1. "What do you suppose Ronnie was feeling right then?"
2. "What might have the dad have felt as he heard that?"
3. "What was the mom feeling?"
4. Make some guesses about what David was feeling as he said, "I want to walk alone."

It is always better to completely "milk" a short story like this with discussion about possible feelings the characters were experiencing than it is to superficially skim over the material. In fact, there is some evidence that superficially skimming over a story can, and does, lead to a surface approach to other people. Anyway it would be extremely helpful if the teacher could write on the chalkboard the names of the four people in the family and, under each name, write as many feelings as the class thinks they were experiencing at that moment.

Any story could be used in this manner. At the first grade level, the goal would be to have the students identify as many feelings as possible for the characters in the story. The point for discussion should come at a time in the story that might be stressful for one of the characters in the story. As a teacher, you might want to vary the narrative so that occasionally the end of the story is at the point immediately following discussion. Or, you might want to finish the story as is indicated by the author. Another possibility would be to have the students in each small group finish the story by telling what they think would be a good ending.

Second Grade Level

Feelings and Behavior

In order to continue the learnings from the first grade level, it would be extremely useful to again ask the groups to list as many feelings as possible. The initial format and strategy would be similar to what occurred in the first grade. But this time the goal would be to learn how these feelings influence our behavior. That is, the way we behave is influenced by the way we feel.

Here is an example of such as initial session:

Teacher: We are going to keep on talking about feelings. I want each group to try to think of as many feelings as you can. Your group leader will write every feeling that anyone in your group thinks of. So what I want you to do is try to think of as many feelings as you can. If you have trouble thinking of any, try to remember some of the feelings *you* have had. After we are finished, I'd like the group leader to raise your hand so that I will know when you are completed, but no group can take longer than ten minutes. Remember, talk *quietly* so that the other groups don't hear your ideas. Go ahead.

Teacher: (allow ten minutes of small group discussion.) Okay, I'd like to hear all the feelings this group was able to think of. Would you read your list, please?

Group Number 1 Leader: Sad, mad, happy, sleepy, angry, eating. . . . .

Teacher: Wait a minute. That's very good, or at least most of them. But is 'eating' a feeling? Anyone, is 'eating' a feeling?

Chorus: NO!

Teacher: Right. But why not?

Class: No response.

Teacher: Eating is something you *do* that comes from a feeling. Eating is something we *do*—we call that a behavior. Anytime we can *do* something, that is a behavior. Eating is not something we feel on the inside. *But* there is a feeling that can cause us to want to eat. What is it? Anyone have any ideas about what feeling can make us want to eat?

Class: HUNGER.

Teacher: Right. Very good. I'm sorry I had to stop you from what you had to say but I wanted to make sure everyone understood that something we do—like eating—is not a feeling. Go ahead group number 1.

Group Number 1 Leader: ahm, let's see. Oh yeah. Tired, and lonely, and I guess that's about it.

Teacher: Very good. Okay, I'd like to hear from this group.

Group Number 2 Leader: Sad, mad, disappointed, sleepy, happy and envious.

Teacher: Okay, very good. Now this group.

Group Number 3 Leader: Looks like we had some of the same feelings. We had sadness, madness, hunger, grouchy, happy, lonely, left-out, sleepy, angry and disappointed.

Teacher: (The teacher may or may not want to write all feelings on the board.) Very good. You all had some really good ideas. I like that. And now we are going to talk about "Why are feelings important?" If I come to school upset and in a horrible mood, would that be important to you? Would it?

Chorus: Yes.

Teacher: Why?

Class: No response.

Teacher: Okay, that's a tough one. So I'd like to see if you could figure this one out in small groups. I want to hear any ideas you have. Don't forget. Don't talk too loud or the other groups will hear your ideas.

After allowing a few minutes for discussion and allowing time for questions, with the teacher and/or counselor floating among the groups, the teacher can conclude:

Teacher: Does any group want to share some of your ideas? Boy, we don't have time to talk more about this but I'd like to have everyone think about this for a week and we'll continue this discussion next session.

Second Session on Feelings and Behavior

The second session on "Feelings and Behavior" may be introduced by reminding the class that the subject is still, "Why are feelings important to us all?" Then, the list of last weeks feelings could be written on the board to remind the class of their previous efforts. Time should then be allowed for students to give their ideas about why feelings are important.

The object then becomes teaching the relationship between feelings and behavior. It might go like this:

Teacher: Feelings are important because among other reasons, they tend to cause behavior. That makes my feeling important to you. That is, the way I behave or act will be influenced by the way I feel. The way I act toward you has something to do with the way *I feel*. And that's what

77

makes *my* feelings important to *you*. And your feelings
are important to me. Why? Because the way you act
toward me and your friends will be influenced by the
way you feel. Remember, *feelings can cause behavior*.
Watch what I write on the board:

Feelings   **Behavior**
1. hungry
2. cold
3. sleepy

Teacher: Any questions? Now I want each group to try to think
of at least three behaviors for each feeling. You can add
more if you wish but try to think of at least three different ways you can act, or behave, if you had these feelings.

If there is some confusion about this idea and the class doesn't
quite seem to grasp what is being asked of them, the teacher
may want to give some more information:

Teacher: For example, if someone is hungry, there are several
ways of behaving as you handle that feeling. We can order
pizza, or ask your parents to order pizza. We can ask for a
peanut butter sandwich. Or you can get an apple. You
can even try to act like you don't have the feeling and
not eat at all.

If this extra input is needed, the teacher may wish to pick
another feeling from the board for the groups to deal with, or it
is possible to let each group pick its own "extra" feeling.

There are several possible follow-up sessions that
strengthen this general idea. One interesting twist would be to
list three *behaviors* and ask the class to make some guesses
about what feelings were influencing those behaviors. If this
type of follow-up is used, "neutral" behaviors should be used in
the classroom at least initially. Then, additional session(s) may
be used with more "loaded" behaviors; such as (1) name calling,
(2) making faces, (3) hitting, and so forth. There should *never*
be any punitive attitude that is elicited from these activities.
The natural peer pressure of trying to analyse these potential
problem behaviors can, however, have a modifying effect.

Put-ups and Put-downs

The goal of this activity is to further establish the relationship between feelings and behavior. Also, sensitivity toward other people's feelings and how that affects us as individuals is increased. In addition, at least one by-product would be the enhancement of students' self-esteem as students are encouraged to make positive statements toward one another. The general idea is that a "put-up" is some statement *or* action that helps someone else feel better. A "put-down" is some statement or action that tends to make someone else feel worse. Here is an example of such an activity.

Teacher: (Writing the words "put-up" and "put-down" on the board) Okay, class, let's think about what we have been talking about. People's feelings. Yours and mine. And people's behavior. Yours and mine. Now for the next few minutes, I want you to think about these words on the board and let's see which, if any, groups can get together and think of what is meant by "put-ups" and "put-downs."

After allowing a few minutes for the small groups to discuss the question and spending a few minutes for general class discussion the teacher may want to summarize and then furtherr stimulate the activity.

Teacher: That's right. Put-ups and put-downs have to do with our feelings. Yours and mine. A put-up is something that someone *says* or *does* that ends up with another person *feeling better* because of what was said or done. A put-down is something that someone *says* or *does* that ends up with another person *feeling worse* because of what was said or done. Has anyone here had any put-ups or put-downs done to them this past week? What were some of them—but don't use the name of the person who was responsible.

Chad: I was called fatso yesterday.

Teacher: Okay, Chad, how did that make you feel?

Chad: Bad, real bad. Like I was real dumb and there was something really wrong with me. Like I wasn't any good—for anything. I felt so bad that I even missed sixteen math problems.

Teacher: Okay, Chad, thank you. Has anyone had any put-ups this past week? This time you may use the other person's name.

Natalie: This morning on the way to school Denise said that she really liked my new hairstyle and that she thought it was pretty.

Teacher: How did *that* make you feel, Natalie?

Natalie: Boy, really great. I was worried that my friends would think my hair was ugly. I was almost afraid to come to school this morning, but Denise really made me feel a lot better.

Teacher: Very good. Thank you, Natalie. And thank you, Denise, for making Natalie feel better. Whenever one of the students feels better, well, it sort of makes my job easier and I feel better. Denise, did you have any idea that Natalie felt that strongly about what you said?

Denise: No.

Teacher: Now I would like you to think of as many put-ups as you can that have happened to you or that you have given to someone else this past week. Don't forget, you may use the names of the other person.

Depending upon the needs of the class, it may be desirable to repeat this activity for the next session and again later on in the year. This may be particularly true if there is difficulty with social relationships.

Stories

At this level, very brief stories about various situations could be read to the class. For example, the teacher could read a story about "Bob and Tom."

Tom said, "Boy, I'll never understand Bob. He used to act nice to me. But ever since I was elected captain of the basketball team, he doesn't even talk to me anymore."

1. Try to think of as many feelings as you can that might have influenced Bob's behavior.
2. Is there anything that Tom could have done to make Bob feel better? Try to think of some put-ups that may be helpful. Would they help?

By the way, these same questions may be used as activities with material taken from characters in reading books and later on, with some practice, from real, actual situations that take place within the social milieu of the classroom and playground.

Being a Friend

This activity has roots in the put-up and put-down activity. Instead of asking students to describe how others have made them feel good, the task is reversed. That is, the students are now to describe ways they use to show other people that they would like to be a friend. Instead of focusing on what other people do toward you, the focus is now on what you do toward other people, with the emphasis being acts of friendship. Possible discussion questions include: Did it work? Did it make them feel better? Here is one way the activity can be started:

Teacher: Remember when we talked about put-ups and put-downs? You remember that we talked about the way *someone else acted* toward you that made you feel better. In a way, we want to turn things around and talk about ways *you behave* or act toward someone else. Only this time we want you to think of ways you would act toward someone else—what you would do or say—to let them know you want to be their friend. It's a lot like put-ups because it's hard to want to be someone's friend without making them feel better. Let's see which group can think of the most ways to "be a friend" (writing on the board). Don't forget, talk quietly so that only your group can hear your ideas.

Inside-Outside

The object of this activity is to identify possible feelings within small groups of selected magazine pictures of doing something. The teacher may choose the pictures for the small groups. It is also fun for the small groups to have magazines and to select their own pictures of people doing something. One way of doing this would be to have the same number of pictures being selected as there are students in the group so that each student is able to select a picture.

After selecting pictures from magazines, the small groups are then to make some guesses about possible feelings the character(s) are having that are influencing what they are doing in the pictures. Then, someone from each small group shows the rest of the class the pictures that were chosen and the feelings the group guessed the character(s) in the picture might be having. If there is time, it is also possible to have the entire class make its contribution after each picture has been described.

Here is an example of the way it could be introduced:

Teacher: Now we are going to try something a little different. I am going to give each group five magazines, enough for one magazine for each group member. Then I want each one of you to pick out some picture in the magazine of a person, or group of people, doing something—it can be anything. After each of you have picked out a picture, the rest of the group is to try to make some guesses about what feelings the person or people *may* be having. After you are finished, the person who has picked out the picture will show the rest of the class your picture *and* tell the feelings that your group thought the person or people might be having. Any questions?

Simon Feels

The object of this activity is to make a "Simon Feels. . ." statement by the teacher with the members of the class showing some action that might come from the feeling. For example, if the teacher says, "Simon Feels *SAD*," then the individual class members would pose like a statue with some action that would come from the feelings.

This activity could have two segments. Although the class would be separated into small groups, the first portion of the activity consists of the teacher saying several "Simon Feels. . ." statements with individual students posing like a statue that shows the feeling. The second portion would then consist of the small groups discussing each feeling the teacher indicates and having one group member showing the pose each group agrees on. Here is an example:

First portion:

Teacher: The game we are going to play today is just a little different. We are going to play "Simon Feels." I am going to say, "Simon Feels *something*" and I want you to pose like a statue showing some action that is caused by the

82

feeling. For example, if I say "Simon Feels *HUNGRY,*" I might go something like this (teacher showing a pose with the hands on the stomach with the mouth open, acting hungry) or I might go like this (teacher smacking lips, like drooling over good food). Any questions?

Second portion:

Teacher: Now we are going to do the same thing ONLY each time I say a "Simon Feels *something,*" each group will talk it over and agree on a pose, like a statue. Then someone from each group will show the rest of the class what pose you have agreed on. I will say five feelings so that everybody in each group will have a chance to show the pose that the group has decided on. Any questions?

Faces

This one is similar to "Simon Feels" and would be an excellent follow-up activity to "Simon." There are enough differences not to make the activity seem repetitious. The teacher gives each group a list of three or four feelings. Then the groups are to discuss the matter and agree on facial expressions that show what feeling is being depicted. No group knows the feelings of the other groups. Then each group takes turns showing the rest of the class their agreed upon facial expression. The rest of the class tries to guess the feeling that they are showing through the facial expressions. One way of starting the activity could be:

Teacher: Remember the game "Simon Feels?" What we're doing today will be something like that, but this time I am going to give each group a list of four feelings. No one else will know which feelings your group has. So, as you talk about it, talk very quietly so no one else will hear *your* feelings. Anyway, after I give each group their list of feelings, I want each group to agree on a facial expression that shows the feeling. For example, if I would have the feeling sleepy, I might look like this (feigning a yawn). After each group agrees on a facial expression, either some*one* from your group, or *everyone* in the group will show the rest of the class your "face." You can either pick one person or the whole group can do it—it's your choice. *Then*, the rest of the class must guess the feeling you are showing. I'll keep track of how many guesses it takes for each feeling.

One interesting way of modifying this game would be to have each group member show a different "face" for the same feeling, with the rest of the class getting just one guess for each "face." The fun part then becomes finding out which face is the one to give the rest of the class the correct clue.

Decks of Cards

Small groups could spend several sessions making their own decks of cards. Each group should make two or more decks out of some type of paper, such as construction paper. One deck would be a "feeling" deck and could have the name of a feeling on each individual card. The other deck(s) would be a "behavior" deck and would have some behavior listed on the deck. It would be fun and would add to the creativity of the activity if each group would illustrate with some picture or drawing (magazine pictures can also be used) some action describing and showing the behavior listed on the same card. Small groups can then trade decks of cards and attempt to put together the "feeling" and "behavior" cards that the original group had in mind. Each group can then tell the rest of the class how *they* think the cards should be matched.

There are several possible variations to this game. One way could be spent trying to fit as many "behavior" cards (with two or three decks of "Behavior" cards) with each card out of a deck of "feeling" cards. It is also possible to match as many "feeling" cards (with two or more decks) with each card from the "behavior" deck. An example:

Teacher: I have given each group some paper that has been cut into card-sized pieces. Each group has two decks. I want each group to use one deck to list one feeling for each card. The other deck is to be used for some behavior, or action, for each card. As you think of each behavior, try to make sure that it can be caused from some feeling you have picked. After you have finished, I want each group to trade both decks of cards with another group. Then each group is to try to match each card with the way you *think* the other group thought of the cards. Any questions?

Chip Trading

The object of this activity is to match everyone in class with three names that are selected out of a hat. Everyone has the names of three other classmates and has been selected by three other peers. Then all students have as a task to make three chips for each name they have picked at random. On each chip is one characteristic about the person that is liked and admired. So we have every student having nine characteristics written on nine chips by three classmates. These characteristics are positive in nature. Although the group leaders may help the students with writing down the name of the positive characteristics, this is more of a class activity than it is a small group activity.

When this is finished, each student in class takes turns being in front of the rest of the class. The positive stroke chips are then read by the students in front of the rest of the class. Here is one way of starting.

Teacher: I am going to put everybody's name in this hat three times. Then each of you will draw three names. If you draw your own name, put it back. Don't let anyone else see your names and don't say who you have. For each name, you will have three chips (pieces of paper) and I want you to write down three things you like and admire on the chips. After you have written down three things for each of your names, raise your hand so I will know you are finished.

After completing this portion, have each student take turns being in front of the class, taking turns at having their chips read to them.

Cupped Puppetry: Approaching People

For this activity, old, used soap bottles and new, unused plastic coffee cups that are inserted into plastic coffee cup holders are needed.

The body of the puppets will consist of the old soap bottles. Holes should be cut in the bottom of the bottles so that students hands can slip inside. Holes should also be cut on the top of the bottles so that the thin, plastic coffee cup inserts can fit inside. The plastic cups will be the heads of the puppets and will be interchangeable throughout some of the activity.

The activity first consists of each small group identifying five feelings. Then, for each feeling, the group will decide on a facial expression to be artistically expressed on the head of one puppet head. Each feeling will also be written down on a separate slip of paper. At the end of this portion of the activity, each group will have the names of five feelings on separate slips of paper and on facial expressions of puppet heads.

At the end of this portion of the activity, each small group will take turns showing a small skit in front of the rest of the class. That skit will have several parts:

1. One volunteer (teacher, group leader or class member) who will act as the person that the puppets will approach.
2. Each small group member, other than the volunteer, will take turns "approaching" the selected person with a puppet.
3. One small group member will toss slips of paper into the open head of the puppet, or the coffee cup. When the person who is holding the puppet reads the feeling that has been slipped inside the puppet's "head," that student will change the head of the puppet so that the facial expression matches that of the feeling.
4. Then, after the student has changed heads, the puppet will show some behavior toward the volunteered person that reflects the feeling that has been slipped into the "head."
5. The puppet cannot show physical contact toward the other person.
6. At the end of the brief demonstration, the student guiding the puppet will tell the rest of the class what the puppet was doing to the person.
7. The rest of the class may either guess the feeling of the puppet, or the student may want to tell the class what the puppet was feeling as the class is told what behavior was being shown.

Strengthening "Feelings and Behavior"

This activity would require at least two sessions. The first session might be utilized by the teacher giving each small group a list of three or four feelings. Each group would be given a different list of feelings. Then each group would have as a task trying to think of as many behaviors as possible that might be caused from each of those feelings. At the end of this small group work, one person out of each group would report to the rest of the class what they had discussed. Each time a small group leader would discuss a certain feeling, the teacher should encourage the rest of the class to add to the list of what that group thought of.

The second activity would be similar to the first. This time the teacher would give each small group several behaviors. Again, each group would have a different list of behaviors. This time the task would be to think of as many feelings as possible that might contribute to that behavior.

Behavior Analysis

At first, make believe situations that resemble real life can be described by the teacher. Then these situations can be "analyzed" by small groups. Artificial situations can be made up by the teacher. For example:

Cory and Kim

Cory and Kim were both third grade students. Sometimes Cory took the ball out for recess. Sometimes Kim did. When Cory took the ball out for recess, he would never let Kim play. When Kim took the ball out for recess, she would never let Cory play. One of the things that everyone noticed was that Cory and Kim both made fun of the other team, and laughed at them if the other one took the ball out.

(1)   What was Cory feeling when he wouldn't let Kim play ball? What did Kim feel when Cory wouldn't let her play?

(2)   What was Kim feeling when she wouldn't let Cory play ball? What did Cory feel when Kim wouldn't let him play?

(3)   What was the one feeling when they were making fun of the team the other one was on? What did the team feel

like?

After several of these behavior analysis sessions that are tried out on make-believe situations, the same principles can and should be used on actual situations that occur on the playground, in the lunch line and in the classroom. Not only does this strengthen the relationship between feelings and behavior, but it also helps sensitize students to the feelings of their peers. If, for example, the teacher is aware of a situation on the playground that happened during recess, the minute the students come in from the playground, that moment should be considered an opportunity to seize the "teachable instant." The students should sit down in their small groups and the feelings of *all* participants and observers should be completely "milked" much in the same manner that "Kim and Cory" were.

A Picture Dictionary For Third Grade Students

The goal of this activity is for each student to work individually within the small groups on a dictionary that defines feelings. The "definitions" consist of writing out what each student thinks the words mean *and* drawing a picture (there may be an option of cutting and pasting pictures from old magazines) of the feeling. Each dictionary would consist of ten feelings, five of which are chosen by the teacher and five of which are chosen by each student. There are two sessions. The first session would be composed of the students working on the same teacher-selected feelings. The second session would involve the student-selected feelings. Here is one way it can be introduced.

Teacher: Today we are going to make a dictionary. You all know what a dictionary is. A dictionary tells you what words mean. I am going to write five feelings on the board (such as excited, scared, happy, embarrassed and lonely) and I want each of you to make your own dictionary of these five words by telling what these feelings mean and by drawing a picture that shows some behavior that is caused by the feeling. If you would rather, you can use these magazines to cut out pictures of some behavior that the feelings cause instead of drawing a behavior. Any questions?

After this portion of the activity, the students can read and show their own dictionary to the rest of the class. Also, the next session can be spent in the same way, only with the students selecting the feelings for their dictionary.

Being a Friend

The teacher writes down several feelings on the chalkboard for the whole class to see. Some examples of the type of feelings might be:

> making me feel important
> feeling like I can trust that person
> feeling like I can have whatever that person owns—
> what's his is also mine
> making me feel like I am accepted for me, with all my faults and good points
> making me feel that I am that person's *best* friend, that I am the "one and only" friend
> not feeling that I have to prove I am really *good* at something for that person to like me. For instance, if we went bowling, I would not feel that I had to outperform the other person
> when that person does something, I get the feeling that how I feel is really considered
> add others to your list

After writing down some of these types of feelings on the board, the teacher can ask the small groups to: (1) tell what behavior on the part of a friend would be needed for you to feel that way and, (2) Rank these feelings in terms of what you want out of someone who is your friend.

Discovering

The goal of this game is to increase communication among classmates and to "discover" some aspects of other students. This is a fascinating way of opening up communication among these students. The emphasis should be placed upon communication and the discovery of information—not mere statistics. Each small group would be a "team" and each team is to complete a list that is given by the teacher. The task is to identify who "belongs" to some of the items. Some sample items are:

—Who has a dog named Caesar? Try to determine
HOW happy the person is who owns the dog.
—Who has the most brothers and sisters in this class?
What are some behaviors that that person likes
the most about what some, or one of the
brothers or sisters does?
—Who are only children? How do each of them
really feel about being only children? What do
they miss most about not having brothers and
sisters? What would they hate to give up if
they did have brothers and sisters?
—Who is really trying to make some new friends in
this class? Do those people feel like their
attempts at making friends are working? Are
they as successful as they would like to be at
making new friends? Who did they try making
friends with? What happened?

There are many possible variations to this activity. In
addition to changing teams, it is also possible to change some of
the items to be "discovered." But the emphasis should always
be on interpersonal communication and how people feel, not
which team wins. After this portion of the activity is completed, it is again helpful to have the participants discuss with
the rest of the class what they have "discovered" and about
whom.

Known and Unknown Friends

First of all, this activity should not be considered a "one
time only" affair. It should be repeated at later grade levels as
well. Obviously, as students are familiar with this activity, some
modifications may need to be made. But most of the modifications at later grade levels have to do with a need for less explanation, not more explanation or different explanation. So a
familiarity with this activity would be sufficient for usage at a
later level.

In introducing the idea of known and unknown friends, it
is usually a good idea for the teacher to write the words
"known friends" and "unknown friends" on the chalkboard.
Then the small groups would be asked to define what the two
terms mean and how they are different. After a few minutes of

discussion, the teacher could then ask the group leaders to summarize what their group indicated. The task of the teacher is to attempt to synthesize the various ideas by suggesting: (1) A known friend is someone whom you like as a friend and both of you know you are friends. Your friendship is *known* to both of you, (2) An unknown friend is someone that you would like to be friends with but you aren't quite sure how he or she feels. You would like to be friends but you *don't know* where you stand.

Each student is then instructed to write down four names of classmates who are *known* friends. Then, on another piece of paper, each student is asked to write down the names of four *unknown* friends. After the students have made their lists, the students are then asked to pin the list of unknown friends on their shirt (or hold them up) and to walk around the room making sure that each of their unknown friends has seen it. The teacher could describe this part of the activity this way:

Teacher: After you are finished with your lists (giving them time to finish before these instructions), I want each of you to hold up the list of your unknown friends and walk around the room and make sure all your unknown friends see their names. We aren't going to do this for your "known" friends because most of you already know who they are. You can talk to them after class if you wish, but right now we are interested in working more on your *unknown* friends. Go ahead, but there is *no* talking allowed during the time you are walking around.

After the students are finished with this portion of the activity, they should return to their seats. The teacher could add:

Teacher: From now on, at least for awhile, we are going to do some additional work on your "unknown" friends. This does not mean that your "known" friends are not important; rather, since you *know* more about your known friends, we don't need to spend as much time on that area. And since you would like to be better friends with your 'unknown' friends, we are going to try to help that along. Now, you remember that feelings cause behavior *and* that there is more than one way of acting if you have a certain feeling. So, as we use what we have learned about feelings and behavior for our unknown friends, it would look something like this:

Feelings **Behavior**
Wanting to be better friends with your
unknown friends.

Teacher: (continued) Now, I want each of you to think of ways you can handle this feeling toward your unknown friend. Your assignment for the next week is to figure out some way to handle that feeling and to try to make your "unknown" friends more "known" to both of you. Does everyone understand what you are to do? Any questions?

The second session on "Known and Unknown Friends" could begin with the small groups discussing among themselves their assignment and explaining to each other what they did to handle that feeling.

After spending a few minutes doing this, the teacher can ask each student to stand up and tell the rest of the class who their "unknown" friends were and what they did to make better friends with them. The teacher can keep a running, written record of all behaviors that were tried by the students on the chalkboard, like this:

Feelings	Behavior
Wanting to be better friends with unknown friends.	1.
	2.
	3. etc.

After each behavior is written on the board as the teacher keeps track of the ways, possible discussion questions that the teacher can ask are: (1) Did that work pretty well for you? and (2) How did that work out trying it that way?

Skitting It

A goal of these activities would be to encourage group interaction in addition to reinforcing the behavioral analysis concepts. The teacher could give some situations to role play. Again, as with "Stories" at an earlier level, it is possible to progressively move toward real situations that occur in the class milieu and/or toward other situations that are being studied in the regular curriculum area. Some examples are:

Meg

Meg was in a very small class. There were only four girls in her class and they were all friends. They even had a club that all the girls belonged to—they called themselves the "Quartets." She really felt important in that group and the girls made her feel that she was someone special.

One day another girl came to class and the girls wanted to take her into the club. When they asked Meg if it would be okay to take the new girl into the club, Meg said, *"If she comes in, I'll just quit your dumb club,"* in an angry-sounding voice.

Each small group could role play this situation. But beyond simply reenacting this, or any other situation, an additional dimension could be added that is both fun and helpful. That added dimension could include both the concept of behavioral alternatives and the underlying feelings involved in the situation. It could go like this:

Teacher: I am going to read a story to you about a girl by the name of Meg. This will be a story about a girl who felt that she had some sort of a problem. Nobody else felt that way but she did. Part of her problem was the way she handled some feelings that she must have had. And yet we don't know just what she was feeling but we do know how she tried to handle those feelings, whatever they were. I am going to read you the story and when I am finished I want each group to make up a skit—like your own TV show—about Meg. But I want you to invent or makeup your own ending, something different from the story I read to you. In the ending that you invent, I want you to think of a different way Meg could have handled whatever feelings she had. And I want you to show in your skit the feelings that Meg was having. I want Meg to say, 'I feel. . . . . ,' whatever it is that you think she may have felt. In your skit, I want 'Meg' to talk directly about her feelings. You will have ten minutes to plan your skit and then each group will show the rest of the class your skit. Any questions?

93

Feelings and Behavior Bank

The goal of this activity is to reinforce the connection between feelings and behavior. Fun and interpersonal communication are the by-products. This is achieved by assigning each small group a bank. The bank may be any container, such as a coffee can. The bank contains slips of paper with names of feelings and behaviors on each slip. The task is then to match up feelings and behaviors and for each group to decide on what they perceive to be the best matches.

Here are some examples of feelings that might be entered in the bank:

Hungry	Scared
Embarrassed	Proud
Lonely	Happy
Excited	Disappointed

Here are some examples of some behavioral descriptions that might be used for the small groups to match up with those feelings:

Throwing your arms up and jumping up and down, with a big grin on your face.

Going to the refrigerator and looking for some milk.

Walking away from the group of other classmates who had just decided to play a game among "the group."

Looking at a test that had just been received and covering up the score so no one else could see the results.

Walking down the halls with a big smile, humming your favorite "Top 40" song.

Looking at a test that had just been received and slowly showing a big grin.

Stopping, very suddenly, and watching a group of boys from the other side of town walk toward you.

Watching a group of students shout with joy over having just been named to participate in a "gifted" class. After watching a few minutes, the student remains by himself and, very slowly, walks away by himself with his shoulders drooped.

There are many variations to this activity. The behaviors and the feelings may be changed, making the issues of connecting the feelings to the behavior more complex. Also, it is possible to have more feelings than behaviors in the bank or,

94

conversely, more behaviors than feelings.

Picture Stories

The teacher may show the entire class some picture and tell a brief story about that picture. The story would consist mostly of a behavioral description of what is happening in the picture. The pictures may be obtained from magazines or some other source that seems appropriate. Then the teacher, or small group leader, would ask the students what each of the story characters were feeling. Here is an example:

ILLUSTRATION 1

The teacher could read this story to accompany such a picture:

Becky is standing at the corner of the building by herself. She has been there for fifteen minutes. Judy is jumping rope and laughing. She is almost ready to break the record for the most jumps. Diane has her back turned to Becky and she is counting the number of jumps that Judy is making. Sue can see both Becky and Judy. She is trying to count the number of times that Judy is jumping rope but at the corner of her eye, she can see Becky standing at the corner by herself. Sue has not told the other girls that Becky is standing by herself.

After such a story, the small groups can be asked these questions. The format can involve the teacher asking the entire class the questions or the small group leader asking the questions within the small group atmosphere. The latter way is preferable. Again, it is desirable to compare the responses of the various small groups.

1. What was Becky feeling?
2. What is Judy feeling?
3. What is Diane feeling?
4. What is Sue feeling?

Fourth Grade

Coffee Cups, Chairs or Whatever

The purpose of this activity is to demonstrate the variability of our interpersonal perceptions and to suggest why that variability is important. We can start the process by using almost any object, preferably of a neutral color. The object is used in order for the class to describe the characteristics of that object along at least three dimensions—height, weight and color. It is important for the teacher to remind the students that, during the activity, there will be *no* talking allowed, but after the first portion of the activity there will be time for discussion. It could start like this:

Teacher: I have four chairs. They are all the same. Each chair is just like the others. I am going to give each group one chair. After I do that, each of you in the group is to look

96

at the chair and examine it as closely as you want. See how heavy it is. Examine it in any way you want. Do this *without* talking. After you have examined the chair, return to your seat and, *without* writing your name on the paper, write down (1) The color of the chair, (2) How tall is the chair? and, (3) How much does the chair weigh? Okay, the color, height and weight of the chair. After you are finished, raise your hand and I will pick up the paper.

After everyone has finished, the teacher's task is to write on the board the number of different ways each chair was perceived under each category. Invariably the spread of responses will be tremendous. We might see something like this on the board:

Color	Height	Weight
/////// /	/////// ///	/////// /

After these results are tabulated, the explanation could continue:

Teacher: We all see things differently. In fact, we all see the same thing differently. Because each of you is different, everything you see, or perceive, is different from other people. And if we all see those chairs so much differently, how do you think we see each other? The way we talk, the tone of our voice, the shape of our mouths, the way we walk and many other ways we "behave." I'd like each of you to look at your neighbor, and other people in class, and be aware that you are seeing everyone in class differently from anyone else. When you think of it, no one else sees you the way you *do*.

When the kids seem to understand the concept of perceptual variability, the teacher can extend some of these learnings to social situations:

Teacher: Has anyone ever seen something on the playground and said, *"This* is the way it was!" only to have someone else say, "No, it didn't happen that way. *This* is the way it happened!" Has anything like that ever happened to anyone here? Is it because someone isn't telling the truth? Or has anyone ever gotten mad at you and you didn't know *why*? Any ideas how that could happen?

The Gossip Game

After allowing time for discussion about the previous activity, another similar activity could be introduced. This activity has the same goal; that is, we want to emphasize the importance of perceptual variability. The gossip game is not new. Yet it fits very nicely with the goals for the fourth grade curriculum. The following structure may be used:

> *The teacher writes a sentence on a piece of paper. The sentence should be of medium length, about 10-12 words.
>
> *The teacher whispers, word for word, that sentence to a student one time in a soft but clear voice out of hearing range of the rest of the class.
>
> *Care should be taken so that the sentence would not have to be repeated. If the listener did not understand what was said, this may be a flexible aspect of the game.
>
> *Each student takes turns repeating the sentence to another student, one at a time, until the entire class has participated.

At the end of this phase of the activity, the last student tells the rest of the class the sentence that was told to him/her. The teacher then reads the original sentence to compare for accuracy. At this point, the teacher needs to emphasize that this is the way many of our messages and communication gets fouled up. Often we assume that what we hear is "true," when, in fact, it only represents another person's perception of what was said or seen. The teacher may ask the small groups to compare this "gossip game" activity with the last activity of 'coffee cups' to see which groups can draw any ideas about how the activities were similar. After allowing a few minutes discussion, the small groups could compare results of their ideas.

Perceptions and Feelings and Behavior

At this point, a small lecture on how perceptions, feelings and behavior are connected is in order. This is an example of the manner in which it could be presented.

> "Remember when we passed out the chairs? They were all the same color, height and weight. But do you remember how many different ways the *SAME* chair was

seen? That's right. We all had different ways of seeing the very same thing. And you would think that if we could see *anything* the same way it would be something as simple and easy as chairs.

But we did not see the chairs the same way. And I knew that would happen. It always does. Because we all see everything differently. Let me say that again. We *all* see *everything* differently.

If you remember what we did last week, you will learn something else. What did we do last week? We learned that we also *hear* things differently from other people. Whenever you say anything to anyone, the chances are very good that that person will not "hear" what you think you have said. It just doesn't happen that way.

So what I want you to think about is this: No one else in this class sees and hears things quite the way you do. In fact, no one else sees yourself the way you do *or* the way you think they might. Your tone of voice, the shape of your mouth, the twinkle in your eyes, the way you walk, the way you look at me are only a few of the things that other people see in you. Even the way you look. Now I would like you to look at the person on your right and on your left and, for the next few minutes, simply be aware that no one else sees you the way you see yourself, or the way you think you are seen."

At this point, it might be helpful to discuss these concepts in small groups. The teacher can ask each small group to think of at least four situations that have actually occurred in which there was some disagreement about what had actually happened. Situations at home, on the playground, at recess or in the classroom can be discussed. After each small group thinks of some real life situations in which two or more people had different versions, the small group leader reports to the rest of the class what had been discussed.

At the end of this session, the point must be made that when two or more people have different versions of a given situation, it is *not* because someone is lying. Rather, it most likely represents what each person actually sees. And since we all see things differently, it is only reasonable that we would perceive social situations differently.

Perception and Feelings and Behavior (second session)

The second session begins to deal directly with the importance of our social perceptions upon our feelings and behavior. This is one way it can be presented:

"Okay, now we are going to discuss why we have been talking about the manner in which we see and hear things. We have a word for the manner in which we see and hear things. Let me write in on the chalkboard 'P e r c e i v e d   S i t u a t i o n.' Does anyone know what that means?

Anything we 'take-in' from other people or from the outside world is a perception. It stands for the way we see, hear or understand information from our environment. And because no one else sees or hears things quite the way you do, we all have a different perceptual experience. Are there any questions about what 'Perceived Situation' means? It stands for the way we 'perceive' any situation. Are there any questions?

Okay, now why have we been talking about this for so long? Why is all this important? Any ideas?

Our perception of any given situation is important because it causes our feelings about that situation. If I perceive Paul as being mad at me and not liking me, then perception will strongly influence the way I feel toward Paul. If, on the other hand, I perceive Paul as being happy and really liking me, thinking I was really someone special, then THAT perception would influence my feelings toward Paul.

Now if Julie is sitting here thinking about how she did on that test she took this morning and is feeling unhappy about it, what will I perceive? I will be able to observe her behavior, the frown, the lowered eyebrows, and I might perceive that, on the basis of the behavior—or my perception of that behavior—she was angry with me. So, even though Julie is unhappy about the test, I 'see' her as being angry at me. And how would that make *me* feel? Now you are getting the idea. So (using the chalkboard), this is what we have learned today.

100

Perceived Situation   ➡   Feelings

Our perception of a situation leads us to feel certain ways about what we perceive. And we remember our feelings cause behavior, so:

Perceived Situation ➡ Feelings ➡ Behavior

So our behavior—the way we act—actually starts with our perception of something we 'see' or 'hear.' Since no one else 'perceives' a situation exactly the way we do, sometimes we see behavior in other people that may be difficult to understand. Are there any questions about this? (Allow for ample discussion and repeat the concept until kids understand how perceptual variability influences our behavior patterns.)"

After this input from the teacher and after the students learn the perceptual variability is important, the class should discuss this together to further strengthen this idea. This is one way it could continue:

Teacher: The other day I went to a fine restaurant and I saw the waiter carrying a thick, simmering, delicious steak. How would that perception make me feel?

Class: Hungry!

Teacher: Right. And what might I do? How would that feeling influence or cause my behavior?

Jeff: You would order a steak. A big, thick, simmering, delicious steak.

Teacher: Right. Or at least that is one of the things I could do. Let me give you another example. Suppose I go to a movie, a really scary movie that makes me imagine all sorts of bad things. If I am still imagining some of those things when I walk out of the theater, that imagination would still be a part of my perceptual experiences. No one else would know that. But how might I feel?

Class: Scared and nervous.

Teacher: You are probably right. Let's say I was still imagining some of those really scary things and feeling a little frightened and scared. . .and then. . . .Erich here comes up from behind me and touches me on the back just to say, 'Hi, how was the movie?' What might happen as I felt that touch on my back?

101

Class: More afraid.

Teacher: Right. And what do you think I might do?

Brian: (Raising hand) Run away.

Christi: Or scream for help (after raising hand).

Jon: (also raising hand) You might act like an ice cube and freeze, become petrified.

Teacher: Okay, you have the idea. And how would *that* make Erich feel, especially if he didn't know I had seen a scary movie? Erich, how would you feel?

Erich: Surprised. Disappointed and embarrassed.

Teacher: Thanks, Erich. Now I want each group to think of a situation like what could have happened to Erich. That is, I want every group to think of something that really happened like what could have happened to Erich. I want every group to think of as many situations as you can in which someone's behavior didn't quite fit the situation as someone else perceived it. My behavior of screaming didn't 'fit' with how Erich perceived what was happening; his asking me how I liked the movie. My screaming didn't fit what he did to me. Now, what I did was alright with *MY* perception, but not Erich's. I was still frightened by the movie I had seen but Erich didn't understand that. All he saw was my behavior. Here is what happened. Watch as I write on the board.

Perceived Situation ➡	Feelings ➡	Behavior
Seeing a scary movie that made me imagine scary things	scared and frightened	Running away (or screaming) when Erich said 'Hi!'

My behavior didn't 'fit' with what Erich did. Again, I want each group to think of as many situations as you can that really happened to you that show the same example.

After this kind of explanation, the teacher should allow questions to assure the class understands the nature of the task. Also, after small group discussion, it is a good idea to have the small groups discuss in front of the entire class at least one or two such situations.

Perceptions and Feelings Bank

The goal of this activity is similar to the "Feelings and Behavior" activity found in the third grade but the focus would be to understand the connection between "Perceptions and Feelings."

Again, a "bank" (coffee cup) which holds a number of possible perceptions and a number of feelings on slips of paper, which have been entered into the bank by the teacher, is used. A spin-off of this game would be to have small groups enter perceptions and feelings into the "bank." These "banks" can be traded with another small group. Then the small groups would attempt to connect perceptions and feelings that have been entered in the bank. Several sessions could be spent on this activity with various modifications. Here are some examples of bank entries:

Perceptions	Feelings
Watching a good friend walk home with someone else without asking you to go along.	Hunger
	Lonely
Watching the teacher hand back a test that you did not study for.	
	Scared
At about noontime, after you had skipped breakfast, you can smell the sizzle of a steak cooking on the grill.	Embarrassed
Out of the whole group of kids who were on the baseball team, you were one of two kids who were not invited to a party.	Left out
	Disappointed
Watching a basketball game being played across the street, and you don't have anyone to play with.	Angry
After dinner, your dad has a meeting to attend and he leaves, your mom is busy in the kitchen and your sister locks herself in the bedroom to do homework.	

Being A Friend

The teacher could write down five personality character-istics, such as:

1. Consideration
2. Truthfulness
3. Honesty
4. Loyalty
5. Generosity

These characteristics could be written on the chalkboard. Then the task of each small group would be to rank in order which is most important, second most important, etc., in being a very good friend. After each group has ranked these character-istics, then a second task can be assigned. That is to define what YOUR PERCEPTION is of each of those characteristics. That is, each group must now define what each of these means.

After these tasks are completed, class discussions may center around these questions:

1. How did you rank the characteristics? Was this a difficult task?
2. What were your definitions of each of the char-acteristics? Was this a difficult task? Which was most difficult for YOUR group?
3. Were there any disagreements?

The point should be made that disagreements are to be expected. Since our perceptions are different, we should not be expected to agree on what each of these characteristics means. In fact, it would probably be a good idea for the teacher to stop discussion before agreement is reached so that this point could be emphasized. Each viewpoint, the teacher should stress, is right; none would be considered wrong even if someone else did not agree with what you thought.

Put ups and Put downs

On page 79, this activity was described for students in the second grade. With our increased learnings about perceptions, this activity should be repeated with some deeper understand-ings. Much of the same introduction could be used with this additional explanation:

Perceived Situation	Feelings

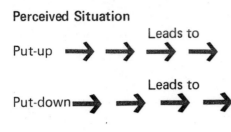

Put-up → → → → Good feelings. Feelings that a person likes to have.

Put-down → → → → Bad feelings. Some type of emotional pain or hurt feelings may be involved.

Each group would then be asked by the teacher to think of as many behaviors as possible that might lead to someone's perception that might involve a "put-up." The task is also to identify as many behaviors as possible that might lead to a perceived put-down. In other words, have each group think of as many put-ups and put-downs as possible.

Perceptions and Behavior Bank

This one is similar to other "bank" activities in the sense that two "entries" must be connected by the small groups. Their connectedness depends upon which perceptions and behaviors seem most related—which tend to go together—by group members.

There is also a second portion of the activity that was not integrated into previous "banking" activities. This time, after small groups "connect" perceptions and behaviors, the groups are to make some guesses about possible feelings that might fit in between the perceptions and behaviors they had put together. As with other banking activities, there are several ways of modifying the game to strengthen these learnings. The complexity of the activity may change. Also, the "Perceptions and Behavior Bank" could be changed to "Feelings and Behavior Bank" or "Perceptions and Feelings Bank" with small groups supplying the missing part of the equation.

Here are some examples of perceptions and behaviors to be entered into the bank:

Perceptions	Behaviors
Standing on a street corner, you see a large dog growling and coming toward you. You also remember the newspaper reports of dogs attacking neighborhood kids.	Turning around and walking the other way.

105

Perceptions	Behaviors
Walking home by yourself with your classmates walking a few steps in front of you. You were not asked to "join in."	Standing very still.
After class, you remember that you had received a test in which you had done poorly. You know your friends had done very well and they were going to talk about the test on the way home. Your neighbor, Jamie, who is also in your class asks, "Do you want to walk home with the rest of us?"	Turning around and walking away very slowly. You ask your friend, "What time is it?" and say, "I have to leave."
You see your mom driving toward school to pick you up to take you for a haircut. It is a beautiful day and the rest of your friends are going home to change clothes to play outside.	

Changing Positions

The goal of this game is to increase awareness and sensitivity of social status we have in the eyes of our peers and what our feelings are about that status. This is accomplished by artificially assigning small group members some preconceived group status. Then, functioning within the assigned status, small groups attempt to make a decision that has also been given to the groups as a task to complete. This activity must be repeated until group members have been able to assume all positions of social status. Thus, if there are five students per group, this activity should take at least five sessions.

Here are some examples of social arrangements that students may be assigned while making some decision:

First Position: You are the leader. Everyone looks to you for leadership for making the decisions. There is no decision that can be made without your approval. You do not create ideas, you only evaluate them.

106

Second Position: The leader likes and respects you and will listen to what you have to say. Because you have influence over the leader, other people look to you to help them influence the leader. Most of the time you are to look at the leader and only look at other people when they are talking to you directly.

Middle Position: If there are five in small groups, there would be one student assuming this position; if there are six students, two students would assume this position, etc. The middle position has some influence over group decisions but only if they can convince the top two positions that their ideas are worthwhile. Most of the time you are looking at the top one or two positions, depending on who will listen to you. You don't look at the bottom two positions unless they can attract your attention.

Fourth Position: Other people in the group will notice what you have to say only if there is a "gap" in conversation. Even then, you can attract attention only if you have an excellent idea. You have no influence over the leader. Your best hope is to try to work through the second or middle positions.

Last Position: Nobody will listen to anything you say. Even if you try to talk, no one will look at you. Nor will your ideas be taken seriously.

Here are some examples of situations that can be presented to the groups for their decisions as they assume assigned positions:

Situation No. 1: This morning, for breakfast, your group has a choice of what to eat. Today, and only today, you have a world-famous chef at your command. He will fix your group anything you want to eat. There are only two rules: (1) Everyone will be served the same breakfast and (2) Everyone must agree on what will be served; the group must decide.

Situation No. 2: The people in your group have inherited a small amount of money. You have enough money so that the whole group can spend all day Saturday doing *anything* it wants. Money is no object for one day but you must spend the money or else you will lose the inheritance. The inheritance means that for one day you can go anywhere and do anything you want but you must first decide what you are going to do.

Situation No. 3: Your group wants to get a mascot. You must decide what animal to get for a mascot and you must decide what the mascot's name will be.

Situation No. 4: Your group has been selected for a very special assignment. You have been asked to represent the student body to recommend to the principal one intramural sport that the student body will have a chance to participate in. There is only enough money given to your school by the school board for one sport. You must decide what the sport will be *and* you must also decide on the reasons you think that sport should be the one selected. Your principal wants to know which sport you think should be selected and what the reasons are for that recommendation.

Situation No. 5: You are the village council on a remote island. Your villagers have never seen the outside world. You are living on a South Pacific island. There is no television, newspapers, mail or any other form of contact with the outside world. As far as you know, the only people that are alive are the natives on your island. There is *no* form of written communication.

Your island has never had any form of schools but you, as a village council, have been able to perceive that your villagers need to learn to obtain more food, protect themselves from wild animals and to upgrade their standard of living. You have just decided to establish the first school that island has ever had. Now your task is to decide what are the three most important areas to be taught in your newly established school.

Situation No. 6: Imagine you are all brothers and sisters. Your parents have just told you that the whole family is moving to another part of the United States. Your family is leaving town. Your parents have asked you to make some recommendations to them about where you would like to move. Your task is to agree on different places in the United States that you would like to live and to rank order which place you would most like to live in, etc.

Other situations may be used. These situations may be reused. In fact, sometimes it is interesting to reuse some of the situations with the group members in different positions. Also, this game should be utilized at later grade levels.

Considerable discussion should be spent within the small groups *and* as an entire class. This should revolve around how this perception of the position you were assigned made you feel. In turn, how did that influence your behavior? Did you act or behave any differently with the various position assignments? Did you feel any differently? Does this help you understand the feelings and behavior of anyone else?

Known and Unknown Friends

On page 90, this game is described. This game should be repeated at this level.

Simon Perceives

On page 82, the "Simon Feels" activity is described. This one is similar to that activity in some ways. For instance, after the teacher says, "Simon Perceives. . . .," small groups would then discuss which feelings would come from that perception. This time, the teacher may say, "Simon perceives. . . .," and the groups would discuss which feelings would come from that perception *and* possible behaviors that might occur as a result of the perceptions and feelings.

Here are some examples of perceptions that can be attached to the "Simon Perceives" statement:

Getting a test back with a low grade.

Hearing your parents talk about getting a divorce.

Watching your friends turn their backs on you and walk away.

At lunch line, you seem to sense that no one really wants to sit by you.

During recess, the team captains are choosing sides and, one by one, as the players are picked, you become increasingly aware that you will be picked last.

During the game, no one throws the ball to you even though you seem to be open much of the time.

It is also possible to add a new twist to the "Simon Feels" activity by extending the process backward. That is, you can have the students make some guesses about possible perceptions a person experienced after the teacher gave the clue, "Simon Feels."

Short Stories

Any story can be introduced and read to the pupils. Social Studies material can also be used. The goal is to provide some sort of follow up to guide the pupils into thinking along the lines of thinking about the reasons for behavior described in the story *or* into thinking about alternative ways the situation could have been handled. Here are some questions that could be easily modified for most situations:

1. What were the perceptions that were being experienced?
2. What feelings did those perceptions lead to? Think of as many feelings as possible that may have been involved.
3. What are some other ways the situation and feelings could have been handled?

Behavior Analysis and Alternatives

On page 87, an example of behavior analysis is given. Real life situations could be used at this level, much like they were used in the third grade. This time, however, the concept of behavioral alternatives is introduced with questions like the above example.

Fifth Grade

Interpersonal Consequences

Behavior has consequences. Specifically, the way we act toward someone else has interpersonal consequences. And the evaluation and understanding of consequences in our daily, interpersonal social behavior are extremely important concepts for youngsters to learn. The initial portion of this activity is to master the understanding of what the concept of consequences means. The first portion of this session would be spent relating the term "consequences" to the behavioral formula and, at that point, teaching the importance of this concept. Then, to strengthen those learnings, we would utilize activities in an attempt to apply the newly learned concepts. This is one way it could be presented:

Teacher: Some of the things about ourselves that we have been learning are perceptions and feelings and behavior. Remember? Our perceptions of social situations cause our feelings that cause our behavior. And now we will discuss *why* behavior is important. Why is my behavior important to you? Why is your behavior important to me?

After some discussion on this issue, the teacher could continue working toward an understanding of interpersonal consequences.

Teacher: Our behavior is important because *all* behavior has consequences.

Perceived Situation = Feelings = Behavior = Consequences

Teacher: Does anyone have any idea what consequences are? Consequences are what your behavior gets you. Every behavior has several, perhaps *many* consequences. Sometimes we get different consequences than we expect. If my behavior of stepping on Johnnie's toes would actually happen, what would be some consequences? The consequences would be his hurt feelings. Just so we'll get the general idea, I am going to write on the board two behaviors and we'll see how many consequences we can think of that might result.

Behaviors	Consequences
Going to a movie	1. Seeing a good movie.
	2. Having fun with a friend.
	3. Enjoying good popcorn.
	4. Laughing (if a funny movie.
	5. Crying (if a sad movie).
Going to the Pizza Hut for a sizzlin' pizza.	1. Good tasting pizza.
	2. Good service.
	3. Prices that we can afford.
	4. Having fun with a friend.
	5. Having hunger go away— getting full.

Teacher: So, if you really understand this, we can see that

111

behavior is also caused by the consequences that we expect to get when we behave in certain ways. Look! What would happen if we went for pizza and got different consequences than we wanted? What if we got:

1. Horrible tasting pizza.
2. Lousy service.
3. Prices we couldn't afford.
4. Because of the first three, we have a horrible time.
5. We are still hungry when we leave the pizza place.

What would happen if, the next time we got hungry, we still felt like we wanted pizza? Would we go back? No, of course not. So the point is that our behavior is also caused by the consequences we expect to get. Yes, the feelings of hunger caused us to go for pizza but so did the anticipation of the consequences. Behavior is complex. It is caused by both feelings and consequences. But right now, I am going to write three behaviors on the board. And I want each group to think of as many consequences as possible that might come from each of those behaviors. Try to think of several.

Behavior   **Consequences**
Going to school
Going out for the soccer
    team
Reading a book

A Throw of Dice

The goal of this exercise is to strengthen the awareness of the relationship between behavior and consequences. But the concept can be extended to other areas as well, such as "Feelings and Behavior" or even "Feelings and Consequences" with the groups discussing which behaviors might intervene between the feelings and the consequences.

First of all, the small groups can spend one session making dice. Each student would make one pair (or more) of dice. On each side of the die would be written a single behavior. On each side of another die would be written some consequences.

After the dice are made out of cardboard or collage, each

112

student would take turns initiating a throw of dice. One student might throw the "behavior" die. Then other students in the small group would take turns throwing the "consequence" die. The task of the groups would be to discuss whether it would be possible for that behavior to result in the consequences that had been thrown. The group's recorder would then write down all behaviors and consequences that had been thrown *and* the small group's idea if it would be possible for the behaviors to obtain that consequence. Class discussion would then revolve around whether the class agrees with the group's idea. After a session or two with the behaviors and consequences being supplied by the teacher, students might want to identify their own ideas for the dice. The teacher could write some ideas on the board for the first session so that students could select ideas for their dice. Here are some suggestions:

Behaviors

1. Eating
2. Running home from school ahead of all your neighborhood classmates.
3. Asking a classmate to go roller skating with you.
4. Walking up and asking to play basketball with some "unknown" friends.
5. If you are new to school, standing by the corner by yourself during recess.
6. Asking your parents if you can have two classmates spend the night this Friday.
7. During lunch line, you ask the teacher, "Do I have to sit by *Julie*?"
8. During lunch line, you are standing by Julie and Jason. Jason is standing in front of you and you try to cut in front of Jason so you can sit by Jon.
9. During recess, the whole team perceives your getting put out. It was close, but they think you got nipped on the shirt. You just KNOW you didn't get hit, so you shout, "You are not fair," and quit the team.
10. During lunch line, you cut in front of Jeff because you thought you got there first.
11. While the teacher is trying to present some lesson, you whisper in Jon's ear some secret you want to tell him.
12. Calling Jon names, like "fatso" or "stupid."

Consequences

1. Letting another person know you would like to be friends.
2. Not having to face the possibility of getting your feelings hurt by some of the kids in your class.
3. Getting full; you are hungry.
4. Having the teacher think you are rude and, at the same time, putting Jon in a position of not knowing what to do.
5. Hurting Jon's feelings.
6. Making Jason upset.
7. Hurting Julie's feelings, like she isn't worth much.
8. Letting your parents know you would like to have a good time.
9. Making Jon feel important but, at the same time, disappointed because you were inconsiderate.
10. Getting to stay in the game.
11. Making the teacher feel you don't care about what she says.
12. Having your classmates think you don't trust what they say, that all you think about is getting *YOUR* way.
13. Feeling good about standing up for what you perceive as being right.
14. Escaping from a situation that has hurt your feelings.

Short Narratives

Short stories can be used with follow-up questions that small groups discuss. The follow-up questions are modified so that learnings are maximized to include the fifth grade level materials. Here are two examples:

BOB AND TOM

Tom said, "Boy, I'll never understand Bob; he used to act nice to me. But ever since I was elected captain of the basketball team, he doesn't even talk to me anymore."

1. Try to think of as many feelings as you can that might have caused Bob's behavior.
2. Make some guesses about what caused Bob's feelings. What was Bob's perceived situation? What was Tom's perceived situation?
3. What are some other ways Bob could have handled his

feelings? What were some other ways he could have *behaved* and still have satisfied his feelings?

4. What would have been some possible consequences for each of Bob's behaviors?

5. Considering the consequences, what would have been the best thing for Bob to have done?

TINA AND CAROL

Tina and her family spent the weekend in another city. They drove to the city Friday night after school and did not return until very late Sunday night. Tina dozed in the car but she did not sleep very well. It was after midnight when she finally got to bed.

Monday morning her mom had a very hard time getting Tina out of bed. But after she got to school, she did see her best friend, Carol. When Carol asked, "How was your trip, Tina?", Tina walked on as if she didn't hear her.

The next day, Tina noticed that all her friends were acting mad at her. Carol told them that, "Tina sure is acting nasty today," and her friends acted the way that they *thought* Carol wanted them to since Carol was *very* popular.

1. Try to think of as many feelings as you can that would have caused Carol to behave that way. Think of as many feelings as you can that would have caused Tina's other friends to behave that way.

2. Make some guesses about what caused Carol's feelings. What was the perceived situation? What caused the other friends to feel that way? What was their perceived situation?

3. What are some other ways Carol could have handled her feelings? What are some other ways the friends could have handled *their* feelings?

4. What would have been some possible consequences for each of Carol's other ways of handling her feelings? What would have been some consequences for her friends other behaviors.

5. Considering the consequences, what would have been the best thing for Carol to have done? Her friends?

Seizing the Teachable Moment

Real life situations that occur on the playground, in the

115

classroom, in the halls and during lunch should be viewed as teachable moments that need to be utilized as educational opportunities. The purpose of these exercises is not to punish anyone. Rather, the goal is to reestablish the perceptual experience of the persons involved; to consider some feelings that may have contributed to the situation; to discuss behavioral alternatives; and to think of possible consequences for each of the behaviors.

The objective is to recreate a real life situation in which there may have been some type of crisis or in which someone's feelings were hurt by another person. At first, the teacher usually initiates these sessions by observing situations firsthand. Then, as students become more comfortable with these methods, students may initiate these sessions. But the teacher must make the students feel that they can also bring up situations that, for the good of someone, may have been handled differently by another person or group of persons.

Even though people MAY be aware of who the participants are, *names are never used during the process*. The objective is to increase social learnings—not to increase defensiveness. The teacher might start out by describing a situation that has been observed, much the same way in which the *Short Narratives* were presented. Fictitious names could be used. Or, the teacher could identify participants as Person A, Person B, etc. The teacher could then tell the story in a similar manner and ask the same type of question that is described in the narrative section. Questions can be easily modified for each situation. During the presentation of such a real life story, the teacher could ask small groups to discuss, in their small group meeting, if any group would like to recreate or role play the situation in front of the class. This would be helpful to give the original participants an opportunity to view and consider behavior alternatives and consequences for those other ways of handling the situation. The role playing is strictly voluntary. While the emphasis should be on behaviorally recreating the situation and alternative ways of behaving, the small groups should discuss the feelings *they thought* participants had. After recreating several ways the situation could have been handled, the small groups should discuss the consequences for each of the ways they thought the situation could have been handled. The role playing should show:

1.   Several alternative ways of handling the situation.
After the role playing, the group should discuss:

1.   Feelings the participants may have had.

2.   Consequences for each of the ways of behaving.

Previous Activities

Some of the activities at earlier grade levels may be easily modified for the fifth grade students. At least the *Known and Unknown Friends* (page 90) and *Changing Positions* (page 106) should be considered for this level.

Inclusion and Exclusion

The teacher could write the words "inclusion" and "exclusion" on the board and ask the class what the terms mean. The next few minutes of discussion could be spent with the entire class by asking, "Has anyone in this class ever felt excluded from something or someone that you wanted to be a part of?" It is possible for discussion to include the *behavior* that leads to the *consequences* of people feeling excluded. After a few minutes of discussing this concept, the teacher would tell a story to further stimulate discussion and sensitivity towards other people's feelings:

Teacher: I know someone who was in fifth grade and that student wanted to invite several friends over to spend the night. But the mother told her she could only have two students spend the night because there wasn't enough room for other guests. So the problem she got into was who to invite and who not to invite. Even though she wanted to invite more of her friends, she finally decided on two girls to invite. So that Friday the girls had a good time at their slumber party.

But the next Monday the girl noticed that some of her friends that had not been invited acted sort of strange. It was as if they were mad for not being invited to the party.

What happened? She only wanted to have a good time. Having a good time was the consequence that she wanted and expected. But she also got another consequence. As she was trying to include some, others felt excluded.

Now the question is, 'Is it possible to include some *without* excluding others?' If so, how do you do it? If not, why not?

I would like each small group to discuss this question and, again, we will discuss each response in class after everyone is finished.

Following-up on Inclusion and Exclusion

After the initial session on inclusion and exclusion, these concepts and increased awareness may be further strengthened by a follow-up session. The second session may be structured by the teacher writing on the board the following:

Behaviors	Consequences
1.	Not having anyone feel excluded
2.	as you try to include one or some
3.	of the group.
4.	

The teacher then sets up a series of situations in which each small group attempts to identify several ways of behaving so that no one feels excluded. Here are some situations that may be used for the small groups to work on:

Situation No. 1: You are walking toward the water fountain. You are new in school and you only know, or remember, the name of *one* of the classmates you are approaching. You want to be friends with the classmates, but you don't know if you should simply say 'Hi!' to the one student you know or you think maybe you shouldn't speak to any of them. You are even considering turning around and walking away from the group that you want to be friends with. You are overcome by embarrassment. What might you do?

Situation No. 2: There are nine people in a group. You and another student want to play a basketball game. But if all of you play, you won't have even sides. What do you do? Think of several ways to deal with this situation.

Situation No. 3: You have five close friends who do many things together. There is a movie this Saturday afternoon that you have all discussed attending. You know all of 'the group' want to go. This Friday, after school, your mom asks you if you want to go to the movie. After you enthusiastically say "yes," your mom tells you that the station wagon is in the garage being repaired and you can only take three friends with you. You really want to see the movie. Think of several ways of handling the situation.

Perceptions and Consequences Bank

This "bank" activity is similar to previous ones described at earlier levels. But this time, as you could anticipate, the focus is upon the broader behavioral framework. There should be a minimum of two phases to this exercise with each phase taking at least one session. This activity can easily be modified and extended even further.

During the first session on perceptions and consequences "banking," the method is similar to previous ones on "banking" techniques. That is, each small group has two "banks," or containers. Within each container are several possible perceptions that have been written down. In the other container, several desirable consequences have been written down on separate slips of paper. Group members may add their own ideas if they wish. One group member selects an item from the "perception bank." Then the task becomes the group attempting to decide which "consequences" the students would want to match up with that particular perception. The process is repeated until all perceptions are depleted. Here are some examples of perceptions and consequences to enter in the bank:

Perceptions	Consequences
You walk into McDonalds for a hamburger when you see some of your classmates and close friends sitting together. They don't see you. You are by yourself.	1. You don't want the friends to see you. You don't want them to know you are alone.
	2. You would like to sit with them but you don't want to be "turned down."
	3. You would like them to ask you to join them.
	4. You want to let them know that you don't like being by yourself and you want to sit with them.
After a test in which you performed quite poorly, you see your classmates	1. You don't want your friends to know how poorly you did on the test.

Perceptions

standing in a group outside school discussing that particular test.

You arrive at school earlier than usual. You see some of the students who usually arrive early standing around the teacher's desk talking and joking with the teacher.

You are in the library. One of your best friends, Julie, is walking into the library with a boy *she knows* that you like in an overly friendly way. From this perception, you feel a sense of jealousy and betrayal.

Consequences

2. You want to find out if anyone else did as poorly as you did.
3. You would like to find out if anyone did quite well. Maybe they would have some study tips for the next test.

1. You want to be a part of the group. You want the teacher to notice you.
2. You don't want to be a part of the group. You are afraid some of the late arrivers, who will be coming in, will make fun of you for being a teacher's pet.
3. You want to go to your desk and finish your homework. What is going on at the desk isn't even entering your mind.

1. You would like for Julie to know that you see the way she is carrying on with "him."
2. You would like for them to know that you see them but you "don't care."
3. You want Julie to stop what she is doing.
4. You want her to know how you feel about it.

These are some examples of situations and potential consequences that small groups may discuss. Also, you can talk about which consequences they would find the most desirable or which ones they might attempt to achieve.

There are several ways of modifying and extending this basic exercise. Students can identify their own "perceptions" to enter in a bank. Then they could talk about possible "consequences" that they might like to achieve. Also, a more advanced form of this activity would involve the inclusion of feelings as a result of the perception *and* ways of behaving to obtain the "consequences" that have been entered in the bank.

Imports and Exports

The teacher could write the two terms on the board and ask the students, either as a class or as small groups, to define what the terms mean. After some discussion, the students should understand that:

1.   **Imports** are those behaviors from other people that, in some way, affect you. You have some feelings about the way another person behaves toward you. You take in the behavior with your perceptions and have some feelings about that.

2.   **Exports** are the behaviors that you dish out to someone else. This refers to the way you behave toward someone else and, based upon those perceptions, other people may have feelings about the way you behave.

After the students understand these concepts, one possible way of increasing sensitivity toward other people's feelings would be to discuss, in small groups, behavioral exports and imports. No names are to be used. Names can only be used if the import or export resulted in a positive feeling. If any negative feelings are involved, no names can be used.

One beneficial extension of this activity would be to ask the students to do a homework assignment. In other words, each student may keep a log of exports and imports. That log could look something like this:

Imports		Exports	
I felt good about what someone else did to me.	That behavior made me feel, in some way, bad.	I think I made someone feel really good.	I may have contributed to some bad feelings.

Each student would have a chance, in front of the entire class, to discuss his/her log of exports and imports. Each student *may* fill out one behavior in each category but there must be a least as many positive behaviors as negative ones. If this is approached in the right manner, it can be a useful exercise in learning. The idea is not to make someone feel guilty. Rather,

121

we want to further sensitize the students toward the feelings of others. If it becomes an exercise in "blaming," our purpose will be defeated.

Conversational Listening

As described on page 53, fifth grade students can begin to learn basic skills required in conversational listening. First of all, using the same example on page 53, the class should understand what it means NOT to listen to another person. This is one way it can be introduced:

Teacher: We are going to talk about ways we get along with other people. Today, and for the next few sessions, we are going to talk about *listening to other people*. Has anyone in this class ever been in a situation, or conversation, in which you perceived that no one was listening to what you were saying. Have you ever noticed that much of the "listening" that people do really isn't listening at all? Let me show you an example of a conversation between two people that really isn't listening at all:

Person A's Statement:	I like the blue dress.	I wonder if my husband will like it.	If my husband likes the dress, I might buy it.
Person B's Statement:	I like the brown dress.	My husband likes brown.	The brown one is pretty, but it is very expensive. I don't think I'll buy it.

Teacher: (Using board to depict point) So, what happened? It was as if these two people were talking to themselves—not each other. It was as if no one wanted to listen to the other. Actually, both wanted to have the other one listen to them SO BADLY that they had to listen to themselves. Let's see what could have happened.

Person A's Statement:	I like the blue dress.	I would love to. But it's expensive and Tom may not like it.	Could be. But I'll talk to him about how much it costs. Say, did you see anything you liked?
Person B's Statement:	Really. Do you think you might buy it?	Hmm. You think he might like another one, huh?	Sort of. I really liked the brown one. It wasn't very expensive. And it's Jack's favorite color.

The teacher could add to this list but the point should be emphasized that listening is a behavior that has consequences. And not listening is a behavior that has consequences. Again, using the board, the teacher could ask the groups to identify as many consequences as possible for (1) listening, and (2) not listening:

Behavior	Consequences
Listening	1.
	2.
	3. etc.
Not listening	1.
	2.
	3. etc.

Additional sessions on "Conversational Listening" can be utilized by: (1) Having small groups think of their own situation and statement and then giving examples of listening and not listening, (2) Having small groups create an entire conversation, like that demonstrated above and on page 122, that demonstrates a short conversation of listening and not listening, (3) Having small groups reenact and role play situations that demonstrate the two concepts in front of the rest of the class.

Previous Learnings

Many of the previous activities are quite applicable for the sixth grade level. Although several can be utilized, at least *Known and Unknown Friends* (page 90), *Changing Positions* (page 106), *Inclusion and Exclusion* (page 117), and *Conversational Listening* (page 122) would be extremely useful at this level. Some of the activities may be sprinkled in between the "Languaging" exercises to help change the routine.

Languaging: First Session

The aim of the sessions on languaging is to increase basic communication skills among our students to aid in their effectiveness in interpersonal relationships. Here is one way to present an initial session on languaging:

Teacher: We have a fairly good idea of how important our perceptions are of other people and how their perceptions are formed of us. We know, for example, that the way people perceive us strongly influences their feelings toward us. Also, your feelings toward other people are influenced by your perception of other people. It works both ways.

Our perceptions are influenced more by the way people say things than by what they say! And this is what we are going to be talking about in the next few weeks. Here is an example of what I am talking about. I am going to write on the board ONE situation and TWO different ways of verbally describing that situation.

Situation No. 1	Statement No. 1	Statement No. 2
Bill is doing poorly in school.	Bill is dumb.	I am disappointed in Bill's performance.

Teacher: Here is another situation that can be described two ways (using board):

Situation No. 2	Statement No. 1	Statement No. 2
Bill is doing very well in school.	Bill is smart.	I am proud of Bill's performance.

Teacher: In both situations, there are two statements reflecting the same perception. Yet the *behavior* of statement number 1 will have a different *consequence* than the behavior in statement number 2. Now, and this is going to be a tough task, I want each group to do two things: (1) if you can, think of the PRIMARY difference between the behaviors of statement number 1 and statement number 2, and (2) think of, and write down, several consequences that might be caused from both approaches.

Situation No. 1

Behavior	Consequences
"Bill is dumb."	1.
	2.
	3. etc.
"I am disappointed in Bill's performance."	1.
	2.
	3. etc.

Situation No. 2

"Bill is smart."	1.
	2.
	3. etc.
"I am proud of Bill's performance."	1.
	2.
	3. etc.

Languaging: Second Session

The goal of this activity is to understand the crucial difference between *naming* our perceptions and talking about the feelings we have about our perceptions. This is one way it can begin:

Teacher: Remember what we talked about the last time—the difference in the *way* we say things and how important *that* is? Today, we are going to try to understand that a little more.

One of the biggest mistakes we make in getting along with other people is NAMING SOMEONE else to describe *our* perceptions and feelings. (You may use the board to show 'Bill's' example.) For example, when we call someone else a name, we are really talking more about ourselves—our perceptions and feelings—than we are the other person. Thus, when we say 'Bill is dumb,' or 'Bill is smart,' we are talking more about the way we perceive and feel than we are about Bill. We need to put the "I" involvement back into our relations with other people. The "I" involvement needs to reflect our perceptions and feelings because the way we talk has certain consequences. Let me show you.

Behavior ➡ ➡ ➡ Consequences
Bill is dumb.
You are dumb.
    or   I am *something (dumb or*
Bill is smart.   *smart).*
You are smart.

Behavior ➡ ➡ ➡ Consequences
I am disappointed
    or   He has feelings of. . . . . .
I am proud.

Teacher: This is a good way to understand the difference. Whenever a statement is started with something like '*you are*. . . .,' or '*someone is*. . . .,' to describe how you feel, you are naming someone else to describe *you*. But, if you start out with something like 'I feel. . . .,' or 'I am. . . .,' then you have a much better chance of saying how *you* feel.

The remainder of this session should be spent with the small groups attempting to deal with and complete the following sequence of "helpful" and "harmful" statements about a couple of situations. The third situation can be filled in by each individual group.

Situation	Most Harmful Statement	Most Helpful Statement
Jeff dropped a pass.		
Brian failed a test.		
3.		

Languaging: Third Session

The third session could be structured by handing out to the small groups a worksheet of statements and asking the groups to indicate which statements are helpful and which are harmful. Here is an example of such a list that could be handed out:

Statement A	Statement B
1. You are impossible.	I don't like all this bickering.
2. I'm worried about your grades.	You are lazy.
3. You are thoughtless.	I don't want to pick up after you.
4. Slowpoke.	I'm afraid you'll be late.
5. That is an attractive dress.	I really like that dress. I wish I had bought it first.
6. I don't feel that I can trust you.	Liar.

7. Think of several situations and make two statements about it: one harmful and one helpful.

Languaging: Fourth Session

A series of situations are indicated below in which small groups can discuss ways to communicate and describe the situations.

Situation	Helpful	Harmful
1. Two brothers are arguing over who gets to be "Captain."		
2. A 12-year-old student has a habit of not doing homework.		
3. Johnny left his room without picking up his clothes.		
4. Sally was one of three girls not invited to a party (have statements from Sally's point of view).		
5. Judy is wearing a dress that seems attractive.		

Situation	Helpful	Harmful
6. Tom is playing around some heavy equipment that has a sign, "Caution: Do Not Play."		
7. The mom sees her son walking very slowly to school and it is already time for the bell.		

Languaging: Fifth Session

The fifth session on languaging could be centered around each small group attempting to guess an underlying feeling when someone makes a statement about something. One way of doing that would be to hand out a worksheet instructing each small group to identify some possible feelings about each statement.

The Statement	Possible Feelings
That steak really looks delicious.	
This sure is a lousy dance.	
That is a good-looking outfit you are wearing.	
That was a hard test.	
That was an easy test.	
He has a sharp-looking car.	
She really is good-looking.	
You sure are slow.	
Each group makes up its own statement.	

Languaging: Sixth Session

The goal of the sixth languaging session represents an attempt to strengthen our understanding about communication skills. In this session, the teacher may ask small groups to identify possible *statements* that would tend to result in certain interpersonal consequences. Here is an example of a worksheet that may be used in this work:

128

Statements	Consequences (other's perception)
	She doesn't like it when I scratch her furniture.
	I sure am stupid for scratching her furniture.
	She doesn't like the dress I happen to be wearing at this moment.
	There is something wrong with my dress. There is something wrong with me for wearing it.
	I sure am dumb for missing that part of the test.
	She really is disappointed over my missing that question. She really cares.
	I sure am smart. I probably am smarter and better than other people.
	She really is proud of my answers on that test.
	Add your own negative consequence.
	Add your own positive consequence.

Languaging: Seventh Session

The following material can be used quite effectively for the seventh session.

The Name	The Underlying Feeling
That steak really looks delicious.	
This sure is a lousy dance.	
That is a good-looking outfit you are wearing.	
That was a hard test.	
That was an easy test.	
She is really good-looking.	

The Name	The Underlying Feeling

You are really neat.
He has a sharp-looking car.
Louse.

Utilizing Communication Skills

The communication skills, both languaging and hearing, may be utilized through practice in structured, classroom situations. It is true that some of the earlier activities on hearing may need some review. But the purpose of these next activities is to give some suggestions in which these communication skills may be reinforced. The rules for using these activities are primarily twofold: (1) anyone may express an opinion AFTER the person who has just spoken has been, in some way, "heard" by the person who wants to say something, and (2) anytime an opinion is expressed, an "I" message must be used, such as "I feel," or "I think." Here are some examples of activities that may be used in this manner. The crucial element is not to place emphasis upon what the group decides; rather, the process of practicing the languaging skills is what is important. There are no right or wrong responses. Every group member's opinion is as valid as any other idea that is expressed.

Space Journey:

Teacher: Suppose you are living in the twenty-first century, when the movie 'Star Wars' could be something that is real. Suppose you are the captain of the spacecraft. The vessel begins to suddenly and mysteriously lose all of the power it needs for a return trip to earth. You have just returned from a long voyage. But now you discover that there is no way the spacecraft can return to earth. Besides the captain, there are ten people on board. There is one small emergency craft that is able to hold five people (besides the captain) and return to earth. The captain is the only one who can fly the small craft and you must go with the five who are to return to earth. Each small group is to imagine that you, as a group, are the captain and must decide who returns to earth with you. These are your passengers:

1. A twelve-year-old boy.
2. A twelve-year-old girl.
3. A fifty-five-year-old minister.
4. A man that no one knows anything about. He has been very quiet during the voyage.
5. A professional football player.
6. A medical doctor who says he won't leave without his wife who is dying of cancer.
7. His wife.
8. A seventeen-year-old high school dropout.
9. A female graduate student who has been tried but found innocent of murder.
10. The captain's son.

Again, the teacher needs to emphasize that 'languaging' and 'hearing' skills need to be used during this activity. Some follow-up sessions with similar guidelines might include some of the following.

Out at Sea

In a session that would follow the "Space Journey" activity, the teacher could ask groups to make another decision. Their task is to now pretend that each group constituted the people on the small vessel that had been saved and were headed toward earth. Each member of each group is a part of the crew that is being "saved." Now, the group faces another decision. The crew has just learned that the landing will occur in the middle of the South Pacific Ocean—about two or three hundred miles from the nearest island. And that island is uncivilized. The decision revolves around what items to take on the lifeboat after the vessel splashes into the ocean. There are several items on the vessel that the crew could take, but there is only enough room on the lifeboat for five items. You must decide from these items:

A knife	A map of the island
Matches	Food
A rifle	An axe
Bullets	Water
Three flares	Extra clothes
First-Aid kit	A stove

Family: Plan Something

Each group may imagine that they are a family that has just discovered that they have four days to spend in any way they want. Expense is no factor because the four days are being "given" to them because they have just won a contest. The only criterion is that the family must agree on how to spend the vacation. Also, before the process begins, it is important for group members to assume familial roles. One useful rule relative to this would be to remember that members cannot assume the role of a family member of the opposite sex. Girls must play females. Boys must play males.

Real Issues

Any issue that is of importance may be discussed in small groups with the communication skills being utilized. One example of this would be "Attention vs. Acceptance."

Attention vs. Acceptance

The aim of this activity is to increase our social understandings while, at the same time, practicing our languaging skills. Here is one way it could be presented:

Teacher: Sometimes we do things because we think people will accept us if we do that. Has anyone ever done that? That is, you behave in some manner primarily because you think you will gain acceptance from other people. Has anyone ever done ANYTHING like that? Okay, an example would be when someone wants to be noticed in class by their classmates. That person doesn't REALLY want to make the teacher mad but in order to get the attention from his or her classmates, he may be willing to ignore how the teacher feels. Sometimes, by acting up in class, you momentarily get the other classmates' *attention*. They look at you. You, for the moment, are the focus of their attention. They might even laugh at you. But, is laughing AT you the same thing as getting their acceptance? Sometimes kids your age assume that when you have the attention of other people, you also gain their acceptance. Now the question is: Is attention the same thing as acceptance? What, if anything, is the difference?

132

Unfinished Business

The goal of this activity is to increase awareness of our own communication patterns. Specifically, we are interested in one area that often results in misunderstanding between people due to poor communication patterns. It could start something like this:

Teacher: Has anyone in this class ever felt that someone else didn't quite understand what you were trying to tell that person? Can anyone think of a situation that has happened like this? Sometimes we can be misunderstood because of 'unfinished business.' That is, we are not given a chance to complete all of what we wanted to say. A telephone call might interrupt our conversation. The class schedule is changing and the bell has rung. Many things can interrupt communicating with other people. But when we are interrupted, that interruption may create some misunderstandings. We aren't allowed to finish our business and misunderstandings result.

After this kind of introduction, the teacher can allow for discussion and examples. Then the activity may be resumed by asking small groups to think of examples to be role played in front of the rest of the class.

How Many

The goal of this activity is to further students' understanding of the complexity of our emotional makeup. In other words, we want the students to consider the complexity of our feelings by having the students ask themselves if it is possible to experience more than one feeling at any one time and, if it is, how many. It could be introduced like this:

Teacher: Now I want you to think of this question: Is it possible to have more than one feeling at any one time? I would like you to talk about this in your small groups and then we'll discuss it after you have all decided what your answer is. This is what I want you to discuss in your groups so that you may report back to the class: (1) Is it possible to have more than one feeling at any one time? (2) What are some feelings that could occur together? (3) What are some feelings that could *not* occur together? (4) Think of some examples *if* you decide that we can have more than one feeling at a time.

Shades

The purpose of this activity is to again consider the complexity of our emotions. But this time the object is to take one feeling and analyze it in terms of its shades of intensity. For example:

Teacher: One feeling such as 'fear' may have different 'shades' of intensity. For example, fear may have shades such as shyness, panic, timidity and downright terror as well as the feeling of fear by itself. Now your first task is to rank order these shades of fear in terms of which is the least intense and which is the most intense feeling that I mentioned.

After the groups spend a few moments with this portion of the activity, the teacher could write several other feelings such as happy, sad, embarrassed and lonely on the board. The task of the groups then becomes to identify as many 'shades' as possible and to rank order those feelings by their intensity.

Chains

The goal of this activity is to suggest the delicate nature of the relationship between the interpersonal consequences of our behavior *and* the perceptual experience of another person. It would be possible to draw on the chalkboard two chain-links with the point being made that the consequences of our behavior oftentimes are another person's perception of us—the way we behave, look, sound and so forth. The chain might look like Illustration 2 on page 135.

The teacher could then suggest that much of what we feel and what we do is 'linked' to someone else.

Teacher: Let's say that Allen was walking down the hall, As he walks past me, I look at him, hoping to catch his eye to say 'Hi!' As I look at him, he doesn't even notice that I am there. Not only did he not talk to me, he didn't even

ILLUSTRATION 2

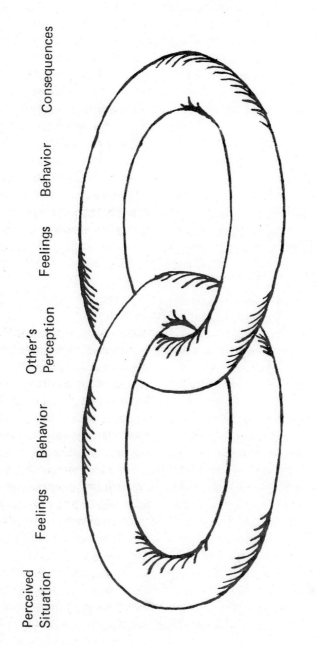

Consequences

Perceived
Situation   Feelings   Behavior   Other's
Perception   Feelings   Behavior   Consequences

see me. In this case, *my* feelings would come from my perception of Allen and how he behaved toward me. I didn't know that he was going over in his mind the test he will be taking the next hour. But the way I behave toward Allen the next time I see him will be influenced by the way I perceived him. And, in turn, Allen will perceive my behavior in certain ways. Now I want each group to make some guesses about the way Allen might perceive the way I act toward him, how *he* might feel and how he might handle those feelings. Go ahead.

After the teacher gives this input to the class, each group can attempt to make its own 'chains' which link together the interpersonal consequences of someone's behavior with the perceptual experience of another. At least two sessions could be spent on this. One session could be spent trying to think of as many 'chains' as possible that would involve the linkage of one set of consequences and perceptual experiences. The next might involve building one chain as long as possible; one that shows the chain reaction of one person's behavior and how it affects a series of different people. Again, these situations the students identify may have been real situations or they can create their own.

Changing Perceptions

The goal of this activity is a simple one. Yet it is an extremely important one in the area of human relations. The purpose is to gain an understanding that it is possible to alter and change our perceptual experiences in social situations. Ultimately, we are the ones in control of our own perceptual experiences. Here is an example:

Teacher: We all know by now how important our perceptual experience is. It has something to do with our relationships with other people. The question I have now is, 'Can you change your own perceptions of other people?' I would like each group to discuss that and come up with an answer. By the way, if your answer is 'yes,' then I want you to give us some ideas about how you think that can happen.

After allowing time for small group discussion as well as general class discussion, the teacher could use Allen (previous activity) as an example before proceeding.

Teacher: Remember when Allen walked right by me without even looking my way? If I were to take that behavior and let my perceptions stop at the behavior, then I would have felt bad. And that would have caused me to behave in certain ways. In turn, Allen would have perceived me in certain ways. That is how conflict occurs.

The point should then be made that in order for us to be able to change our perceptions of someone else, the most crucial element would involve an ability—and willingness— to go beyond what we see. Our perceptions must involve more than just behavior. We must try to make some guesses about what caused the behavior. We must understand, or at least try to understand, the behavior we observe.

Teacher: Even if we are wrong, we must make some guesses about what is causing another's behavior. If I see Allen walking down the hall and he doesn't look at me, I might make several guesses. I might say: (1) Allen is worried whether Jenny will meet him at the skating rink—he's afraid she'll say 'no.' (2) Allen didn't have breakfast and all he could think about was sizzling hot pizza. Now, both of my guesses may have been wrong but at least I tried to *enlarge* the perception of what I saw by trying to understand it. If we try to do that, even if we are wrong, then our feelings don't get hurt nearly so often. And we have a lot more fun.

At this point, perhaps in another session, it would be useful for the students to make some guesses about some behavior that they didn't understand during the past week.

The point should also be made that talking with the other person to find out some of these reasons for a given behavior would be desirable. But this should happen *after* they have tried to make some guesses on their own.

Hearing: Feeling Starting and Feeling Stopping

The purpose of this activity is to consider ways we

respond to people that may have either a "feeling starting" or "feeling stopping" consequence. That is, when people attempt to communicate something to someone else, the choices of responses that we choose may either result in a feeling stopper or feeling starter. Thus, indirectly, this activity involves increasing our listening skills as a method of communication. It would start like this:

Teacher: Has anyone in this class ever had a situation in which you had some feelings that you wanted to talk about? Anone? Ever? (Allow time for discussion.) You wanted to really talk to someone and you wanted them to understand—to listen to *you* and how you felt. When you felt this way, have any of you ever felt that someone else cared enough to listen to what you wanted to say?

Jenny: Today, when I came to school, I felt kinda nervous and all I could think about was this dumb test I am taking tomorrow. I couldn't think about anything else. And Cory noticed that I wasn't acting quite right and asked if there was anything wrong. Even though I didn't say anything, he kind of listened to the way I was acting, if that makes any sense.

Teacher: Sure. And what happened?

Jenny: Well, we talked about the test. And he acted like he really cared about how I felt. After we talked, I felt better and I could think about other things, like listening in class. I know it doesn't sound like much, but. . .I felt better.

Teacher: Thank you, Jenny. What Cory did was listen to Jenny's feelings. Because of what he did and said, we could call that 'feeling starting' because it started Jenny talking about her feelings and that was helpful. (Write the "feeling starting" on board.) Anyone else have any examples of 'feeling starters?'

After allowing for more discussion, the teacher could continue:

Teacher: And has anyone ever tried to get someone to listen to you but because of something they said or did, were 'stopped?'

Class: No response.

Teacher: Okay, but I think you get the idea. The way we act, what we say, how much we care, all tell someone who is trying to communicate something. We can use 'feeling starters' like Cory did. Or we can use 'feeling stoppers,' which tell the other person to stop talking about his or her feelings.

The teacher then asks each group to role play a situation that shows a situation in which someone is wanting to talk to someone else about *something*. The role play situation should have two scenes: one in which the listener shows some "feeling starter" statements and another in which the listener doesn't care about what is being said and shows some "feeling stoping" ways of acting.

Court

The goal of this activity is to continue to build on social skills. To achieve this, mock court sessions could be held with the emphasis being on skill development *and* making people feel better as a result. Thus, for this activity, the teacher will have to seize the teachable moment and spontaneously call court into session whenever one of two conditions are met: (1) If someone's feelings have been hurt because of someone's insensitivity, or (2) When someone has been able to make someone feel better.

During the first condition, "defense" and "prosecuting" attorneys are appointed. The role of the defense attorney is to indicate that the mis-action was unintentional. The role of the prosecuting attorney is NOT TO MAKE THE DEFENDANT LOOK BAD. Rather, the focus is upon the perceptions and feelings of the victim—not the "badness" of the defendant. The line may be a thin one, so the judge (teacher) may have to keep a reign on over-zealous lawyers. The class will be the jury. The defendant may be "sentenced" by the judge (teacher). The sentencing should emphasize some behavior that would make the other person feel better.

This activity, if approached in a sensitive, non-judgmental manner, could help sensitize students to the feelings and perceptions of others. Possible sentencing may include such things as: (1) Walking home with the victim; (2) Holding the water fountain pedal for the victim for a week; (3) Sitting with the victim for a week at lunch; (4) At lunch line, waiting on the victim by getting the tray and accessories; (5) Anything creative and fun for *both* defendant and victim.

The second type of court session may be called by the teacher when someone does something for another person that is positive and helps to make them feel BETTER than before the deed occurred. Instead of a prosecuting attorney, there is a "prescriptive attorney." There is no defending attorney. The role of the "prescriptive attorney" is to magnify the good deed in front of the jury (class) and judge (teacher). Witnesses may be called and sentencing may be passed. If the offender is found guilty of a good deed, appropriate sentencing may be passed by the judge. If it can be shown by the "prescriptive attorney" that the good had an impact on the whole class, by using the "chains" formula, the entire class may be involved in the sentencing. Again, sentencing may include going to the front of the lunch line; being waited on during lunch; and anything that is fun and is taken in that spirit by the class and people involved.

Again, the focus should be the consequences of the behavior involved in the 'good deed' which would include the perceptions and feelings of the person who was the object of the good deed. And if that caused behavior which impacted upon other people, they too may be involved. The perceptions, feelings, behavior and consequences may be linked to as many classmates as possible. It is a fun exercise that shows the degree to which our behavior is "chained" to other people.

Interpretations

This is a communication activity that blends aspects of languaging and hearing. Quite easily and beneficially, several sessions could be spent on this strategy. The method involves presenting a series of statements in which our perception has been named. Then, the object is to make some active interpretations about what the statement really meant; that is, what feelings and perceptions were involved on the part of the sender? For example:

Statements	Interpretations
That is a pretty dress.	1. I like the way you look.
	2. I am attracted to you.
	3. I am jealous of you.

Statements	Interpretations
She's a really neat person.	1. I like her and respect her. 2. I wish I were more like her 3. I wish she liked me.
He really is smart.	1. 2. 3. etc.
He is really stuck-up.	1. 2. 3. etc.
Boy, that is a good-looking coat.	1. 2. 3. etc.

Several modifications can quite easily and beneficially be made from this strategy. Three or four sessions can be very helpful. During the second session, a series of *statements*—about some person—that are similar to the five examples given above can be given to the groups.

The third and fourth session could be spent with the process being reversed. That is, interpretations can be given in which the group attemps to make four statements about that original interpretation or perception. Two statements will name the perception. The other two statements are to reflect true feelings. For example:

Perception (original interpretation)	Naming Statements
Watching your best friend walk off with two very attractive members of the opposite sex.	1. She is really boy crazy. 2. **Feeling Statements** 1. I really wish she would ask me to join them—I feel left out. . .and jealous. 2.
Being unprepared for class, you hear your teacher call your name to answer a question that you have *no idea* how to answer.	**Naming Statements** 1. Why is she doing that to me? 2. **Feeling Statements** 1. I really feel embarassed.

2.

The fourth session could be spent by having the small groups think of their own perceptions and the two kinds of statements that would reflect those perceptions.

Behavior: Satisfying Feelings and Considering Consequences

The goal of this activity is to have the students be able to behave in ways that satisfy their own feelings while, at the same time, full consideration is given to the consequences of that behavior. More realistically, it is probable that this goal represents a level of awareness that would have some impact upon our students' insight, sensitivity and behavior. Obviously, behaving in ways that satisfy feelings and consider interpersonal consequences simultaneously is a *lifetime* goal. It is not reached by a brief exposure in school. But the process can begin at this age level.

The teacher may point out that truly effective behavior is like making a purchase. That is, when we buy an item, we consider how much WE WANT that item as compared to how much it WILL COST us to purchase that item. Behaving in social situations is similar if we are aware of the situation and our feelings.

Effective behavior in social situations considers BOTH our wants and the costs, if any. Here are two examples: At a party, we can see both types of situations. Wild Bill, on the one hand, is the type of guy who does *anything* he wants. If he feels like doing it, he does it. He doesn't care if it hurts other people's feelings or not. He makes fun of people. He laughs at them. He calls them names. Anything goes with Bill. He behaves in ways that seem designed only to satisfy his feelings.

Harold, on the other hand, is so afraid of offending other people that he seems almost immobilized. He doesn't do anything because he is afraid that he might behave in some way that another person might disapprove of. So he does nothing. It's safer that way. He just sits at the table and watches other people have fun. He wants to, but he is so wrapped up in anticipating the consequences BEFORE THEY EVER HAPPEN that he does nothing.

So, we have two cases. One way is overly concerned

about the consequences. The other way is too concerned about the satisfaction of feelings. If we use the analogy of "purchasing and behaving," one person would be a miser, he spends nothing; and the other person would be a spendthrift, he spends everything he has. . .and then some.

At this point, the teacher could ask groups to make lists of behaviors within certain situations that are examples of both ineffective ways of behaving.

Being a Spendthrift	Being a Miser
1.	1.
2.	2.
3. etc.	3. etc.

Role Playing Not Listening

At this point, it would be helpful to simply ask groups to create, and then role play in front of the rest of the class, two situations: (1) A situation in which someone is really listening to another person, and (2) A situation in which two or more people are talking and no one will listen to anyone else.

Probably the most effective way for the strategy to be implemented would be to have two sessions. The first role playing situation would be to create a 'no listen' scene. The second session could be oriented around showing a 'listening' scene.

Hearing Names

The goal of this strategy is to reinforce previous learnings that we sometimes camouflage our own feelings by naming another person. Beyond that, we also want to show how we can "hear" *more* than what someone *says*. It is a good stepping-stone toward active listening presented in the next secondary course. The introduction could go like this:

Teacher: How many people would like to impress another person, make a good impression on someone—anyone? Sure. We all do. Want to know how to do that? You can do that by making the other person feel good and important. It never fails. If you make the other person feel good and important, that person will also feel good about you. Usually, we feel about someone else the same way they make us feel about ourselves.

Anyway, you can make another person feel good by making yourself sound intelligent at the same time. Sound tricky? Listen. Most people hide their feelings by naming someone or something else. We can hear a statement that has a feeling underneath:

Statement	Feeling
(Right before dinnertime)	
It is getting late.	You are getting hungry, huh?

This statement was made right before it was time to eat. Within that situation, the feeling was "heard." If the statement was made before bedtime, the feeling may have been a different one—perhaps being tired or fatigued.

Now, when you 'hear' beneath the name you are doing two things: (1) making the other person feel important, and (2) sounding intelligent. The other person may think, "Wow, how did you know what I was *really* thinking?" But it is really amazingly easy. Let's practice.

Feeling	Statement
	Isn't dinner ready yet?
	What time is it? (Question asked right before bedtime)
	That test sure was hard.
	You sure are slow.
	Can't you go faster?
	You look SHARP!
	That was an easy test.

Secondary Course II

Dynamics of Perceptions

On pages 13-33, material is presented that eighth grade (and older) students can understand on the nature of social perceptions. That material can, and should, be used in didactically presenting these concepts. One or two sessions can be used in covering that important information. Following the presentation of that material, several strategies can be employed to strengthen those learnings.

144

Rejection: Its Pain and Its Effects

The goal of this activity is to sensitize the students to the consequences of personal rejection, both in terms of the emotional pain AND the manner in which it subsequently influences relationships with other people.

The strategy involves the restructuring of a hypothetical social situation and showing, through role playing, how our perceptions lead us to feel rejected. The strategy can revolve around this basic structure:

*A simulated telephone conversation is arranged involving four students.

*One of the students will be telephoning the other three to invite them to his or her birthday party this weekend.

*The caller will telephone the students in a prearranged order. The first two kids the caller asks to the party MUST turn down the offer, giving all kinds of inconsistent and unlikely excuses. The third person that is called must hesitate momentarily, giving consideration to whether or not he or she should attend the party or stay home to be with some relatives coming in from out of town.

*If the caller STILL sounds happy and sounds like someone who seems interested in the third person coming to the party, the third person may say 'yes' to the invitation. But if the caller sounds kind of 'down' and unenthusiastic, the third person may also reject the invitation.

*Chairs are arranged in front of the class so that classmates can observe reactions of the caller. Chairs are back-to-back; that is, the persons 'on the telephone' cannot maintain eye contact.

*Instructions should be given to the three kids being called and the caller separately, out of earshot of each other and the rest of the class.

Discussion is of crucial importance following the implementation of this exercise. Discussion questions include: (1) Did any of the class notice any difference between the caller's attitude and tone of voice between the first and third call? (2) The instructions to the people being called should be brought to the attention of the class and caller, emphasizing the fact that the third person COULD have accepted the invitation IF certain conditions were met.

Points to bring out in discussion include: (1) The caller was acting and sounding as if he/she were rejected BEFORE the third person had a chance to accept, and this made that person want NOT to accept the invitation; (2) The caller perceived rejection before it happened (on the third person) and this caused feelings that reinforced that perception. . .a painful cycle for anyone; (3) Was it fair for the caller not to give the third person a REAL chance because of what two other people had done?

A homework assignment could be given that might provide the basis of discussion for the next session. Specifically, (1) Has this ever happened to you when you were expecting someone to reject you even BEFORE you gave them a chance? (2) Was this fair to that person? (3) What contributed to these perceptions; that is, was it primarily some psychological need state, environmental situation of personal resource, or a combination of the three? (Use the board to show how the three affect perceptions.) Since peer pressure, personal alienation and rejection are such powerful forces at this age, this strategy is of vital importance.

Climbing

This is another perception-oriented activity. The goal of this activity is to gain insight into the manner in which subtle social forces influence students' perceptions, feelings and behavior. This activity can start out by the teacher talking about the various types of social climates that may exist within any given classroom or group.

Climate No. 1: Top Ten exists when students have been rank ordered in terms of their social attractiveness to other students. Ten (or some other arbitrary number) students are the popular ones and are the ones other students gravitate toward. This climate influences the classroom because people are trying to climb into the top ten by a variety of methods.

Climate No. 2: The Bottom Ten exists when the students spend considerable energy avoiding social isolates who, by association, will drag down the social position of persons they are seen with. Students do their climbing by making fun of the bottom ten

146

(or some other number) and shoving them down as far as the ladder will go. Thus, their climb is motivated primarily by the downward push of the bottom ten.

Climate No. 3: Somewhere In Between means that elements of both of the other positions are included. There is a 'top ten' and also a 'bottom ten' and the climb may involve aspects of either.

Small group discussion may involve which climate most closely approximates the current one. Also, helpful discussion might include whether this is beneficial and what, if anything, can be done to change the group climate.

Changing Positions

On page 106, *Changing Positions* is described in detail. At this level, with all the emphasis of social pressure and social functioning, it would be extremely helpful to repeat that strategy. To be quite honest, the fact that this was introduced at such an early level is related to a readiness type of question. That is, earlier introductions were helpful mostly to prepare the students for maximum learnings at this level.

Inclusion and Exclusion

Like the previous activity, page 117 describes an exercise that, for maximum benefit, should be repeated at this level.

Self-Concept: Its Causes and Its Effects

Some of the material on pages 13-33 is repeated at this point. This time, however, the emphasis is upon the development of our self-concepts. The teacher can begin the activity by asking the class what self-concept means. After allowing some discussion, it would be helpful to guide the students' thinking by suggesting that self-concept is the manner in which we perceive ourselves operating within a given social situation. The concept can be graphically illustrated by showing Figure 12 on the chalkboard.

The point needs to be made that the environmental situation in connection with one's experienced personal resources to cope with that situation provides much of the basis of the development of our self-concept. For illustration purposes, the teacher would do well do use the analogy of the caller's feelings and sense of self-concept when rejection was felt from the first

FIGURE 12

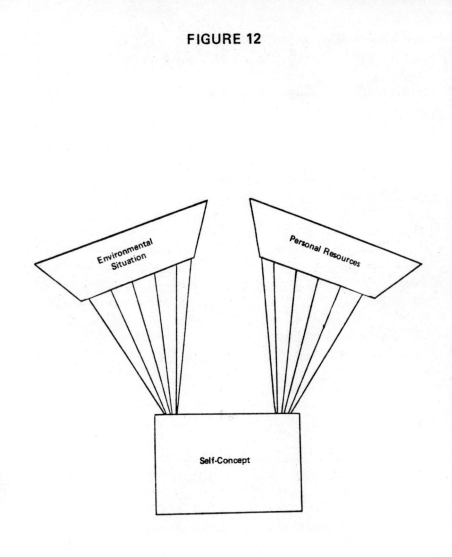

two called and how that influenced future behavior (see page 146). That is, the caller experienced an *environmental situation* (two rejections) and lack of *personal resources* to cope effectively with the situation as perceived. At this point, discussion can resolve around what this did for the caller's self-concept.

Small group discussion can then be oriented around thinking of personal examples in which YOUR self-concept was influenced, either for the better or worse, by a given environmental situation in combination with your experienced personal resources. At least one session could be spent on this one. Usually, the interest is high enough and the discussion is lively enough to spend more than one session on this critical issue.

After one or more sessions on the above strategy, the discussion can take an interesting and fun twist. Now the aim is to discover and understand what influences our self-concepts have upon the manner in which we perceive the environment and our ability to cope. The process and illustration is reversed but the aim is to show the degree in which the concepts are interrelated.

The point should be made that our self-concepts can dramatically influence the manner in which we perceive any given environmental situation *and* our ability to cope with that situation. In any given situation, our perceptual figure may be our lack of self-concept. To the extent that our personal resources and the environment are relegated to the background, our effectiveness in social situations may be significantly reduced.

The example can be given of a boy wanting to call a girl to go skating but because of poor self-concept, he may be expecting a rejection before he even calls. As such, he may not even make the call. Or, if he does, he may stumble through the conversation to the extent that he may actually receive such an expected rejection. Class discussion within small groups may focus upon thinking of other examples that would show how one's self-concept may influence or distract one's ability to perform or communicate.

Attribution

In many instances, we attribute OUR motivations and attitudes to other people. We assume and perceive that they actually hold certain feelings and beliefs. We attribute to other

FIGURE 13

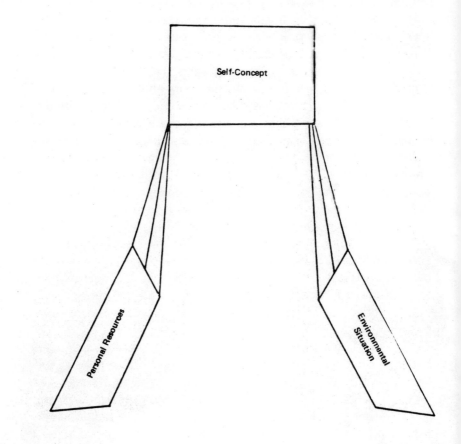

people feelings we assume they have. Often that is a function of OUR perceptual experiences and not the other person's. The example on page 146 and the 'caller's' experience would be one example. When we see a group of peers standing around laughing, joking and talking, we may attribute certain feelings and attitudes to them. But we must remember that this is a result of OUR perception and not necessarily what is going on inside them. Our psychological needs, most usually self-concept, and our personal resources may influence our perception of any given situation and form an inaccurate perception. Based on this, we may attribute certain aspects to that situation. These are, at least in part, the conditions that give rise to our attributing to other people our own underlying attitudes.

Points to be made in small group discussion include: (1) Have you ever, now that you think about it, attributed to someone else YOUR own feelings? (2) How did this affect the manner in which you interacted with that person at that moment? (3) Has anyone, now that you think about it, not given you a chance because you felt they attributed something to you? (4) How did this make you feel?

Again, several sessions could be spent on this very important concept.

Active Listening

The distinction must be made between *conversational listening* and *active listening*. Conversational listening occurs at the behavioral level. That is, you listen to what is being said at face value. This also is an important skill (see page 122). Active listening, however, goes beyond conversational listening because one must actively interpret the feelings that one is experiencing at any given moment. Active listening is an extremely useful skill, especially when someone is experiencing some interpersonal stress. Here are the necessary elements of active listening:

*Not only hearing the words of the speaker, but also actively listening for the feelings behind the words. It is the feelings that you respond to. . . .not the words.

*You must emphathize with the speaker and try also to understand the perceptions of the speaker as well. Thus, you listen not only for feelings, but also for perceptions. well.

FIGURE 14

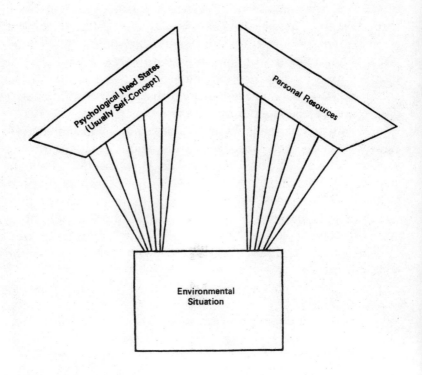

*You must not judge what is being felt or perceived as "good" or "bad;" rather, your role is to try to understand the other person and the stress that is being experienced.

*Some key phrases involved in active listening include "you" statements. Statements such as, "you mean . . . .," "You think. . . .," "You feel. . . .," and "You are saying. . . ."

*The "you" statements are a tool to help focus upon the other person's feelings and perceptions.

After the students understand the basic skills required in active listening, students may be arbitrarily assigned to groups of three students each. Within each group, there will be three respective roles: (1) the speaker, (2) the listener, and (3) the observer. During the first session, each student will trade roles so that everyone can be assigned to each position. The most important role is the person who is actively listening to the one who is experiencing stress.

Here are some sample situations and initial statements to begin the role playing:

Situation	Statement
During final exam week, you are in a class that has just received results of a test from the school's most difficult instructor.	That was one of the most stupid tests. I hate that teacher.
This Friday it is Jeff's birthday. Jeff is one of the most popular boys in class. He has just sent out twelve invitations—six boys and six girls —to his birthday party.	Who cares about Jeff? He's just a four-eyed fatso.
Next week, basketball season starts. Tonight the coach will post the names of the boys who have made the team. Twenty players are out. Only	He's a lousy coach. He doesn't know anything.

ten can make the team.

The speakers should be encouraged, before assuming the role, to become sensitive to the role that is being played. They should be encouraged to think of some feelings, and more than just the 'obvious' ones, and perceptions that go along with the situation and to identify with them. The role of the listener is to attempt to uncover and understand what they might be.

Some examples of additional information that the listener should be unaware that the speaker could assume might be:

Situation No. 1: No one knows that you are trying out for a scholarship. This is your senior year and unless you can qualify for the scholarship, you won't get to go to college next year. You are afraid of not doing well enough on this test and are concerned that you might not get to go right on to college. But you have made up your mind that if you don't do well, you will work for two years and save money that way for school. You have already been accepted by the school of your choice and you are afraid, if you lose this opportunity, you may not get a second chance.

Situation No. 2: Jeff is one of the friends that you feel close to but you don't feel that you are as popular as some of the other friends that Jeff has. You are really concerned that you are losing Jeff as an important and much-valued friend.

Situation No. 3: Your dad was an excellent basketball player. He has been talking all week about how much he is looking forward to going to see the games so that he can watch you play. He even changed work schedules to be able to watch you play. And now you are really afraid that you won't make the team. You are really anxious and nervous and you are feeling considerable pressure.

The role of the listener may be to actively listen to the problems of the speaker. It would be interesting to see which of the active listeners would be able to uncover this unknown information through their active listening. The task is not to embarrass those who did not uncover this information but to learn from those who did.

Those more successful at active listening could demonstrate their skill in front of the class by reenacting the previous active listening role. Additional sessions may be held with various situations and hidden information being supplied by the teacher or by the students themselves.

Secondary Course III

Typical Reactions to Stress

First of all, students should be clear as to their understanding of what stress is. Interpersonal stress is defined as coming from a perception which the environmental situation, personal resources or psychological need states are contributing to a disruption in a person's feelings and behavior. The chalkboard can be used to show that stress may be invisible and it isn't always possible to SEE the source of stress. For example, we cannot observe the psychological need states or the person's personal resources so we don't really know when a person is experiencing personal stress.

The only thing we can go by to determine if a person is experiencing stress is the behavior that we see. There are three basic kinds of stress reactions: (1) blaming, (2) ignoring, and (3) surrendering. The examples and concepts discussed on page 45 would be very helpful here. The students should have a clear understanding of what blaming, ignoring and surrendering mean before continuing.

Assuming Positions

During this same session, all students are assigned to a group of four. There must be boys and girls in each group. Students are then asked to assume one of the positions; blaming, ignoring or surrendering. No one else is to know which position another person has assumed. After the students have secretly assumed one of the three positions, the teacher gives the groups a task to work on in which each student acts out the position he or she has assumed. Each group is to try to make a decision with each student playing the role of the position that has been assumed.

Three sessions could be spent on this strategy, with each student assuming a given position for each session. *Space*

155

Journey, Out at Sea, and *Family: Plan Something* are described on pages 130-132 and could be used for these purposes. Each activity could represent a session for each assumed position.

Handling Stress: Who, if anyone, Owns the Problem

The first step in learning to deal with stress involves understanding who, if anyone, owns the problem. Now, obviously, there are complicating factors because it is possible for someone to experience stress when it can't be seen by another person, except to make some judgment on the basis of that person's behavior. But the concept is still important and is helpful because it strongly affects which one actually deals with the stress. Here is a format that is useful in the following exercises in discussing who, if anyone, owns the problem:

You own the problem	Other person owns problem	Isn't any problem

Subsequently, a series of situations can be given to each small group. In turn, each group would decide about "who" owns the problem. Here are some examples of the type of situations that may be used:

At school, another student is leaning up against your locker and, unknowingly, his pencil is gouging a deep mark in your locker.

Your younger brother tagged along with you as you went to one of your friends' homes to study for a test. Now he is pulling at your shirt, asking, "Are you ready to go home yet?"

One of your friends is driving your new car too fast and too recklessly.

Someone comes and complains that a test was too hard and the questions were not fair.

You are the parent. Your teenage son wants to borrow the car. And you have a meeting you MUST attend that night.

Your younger sister hasn't fed the cat. You know that
you will be stuck with her duties if she sluffs off.

Someone keeps interrupting a conversation you are trying
to have.

Someone asks, "Where is the restroom?"

At a football game, you see a lot of students becoming
very excited.

You have misplaced your notebook.

Your younger brother has just spilled milk at breakfast.

Your dad is wanting to do some work on the car but he
can't find the tools. You were the last to use them.

You walk in with mud all over your feet. Your mom has
just cleaned and scrubbed the floors.

You see your girlfriend walking home with another guy.

The point should be emphasized that if there isn't any
problem, conversational listening and talking are quite appropriate skills. But, at the same time, if there is someone who is
experiencing stress, different skills are needed to handle the
stress depending on who owns the problem.

When Other Person Owns Problem

When someone else is experiencing stress, active listening
is an appropriate and useful skill to utilize. One way to learn
and experience the meaningful nature of active listening would
be to dramatize in a role playing type of situation methods of
dealing with someone else's stress or problem. Each small
group could dramatize the reactions of: (1) blaming, (2) ignoring, (3) surrendering, and (4) active listening. One session could
be spent dramatizing each respective reaction. Here are some
possible situations that could be dramatized:

1. You are standing in the hall by your locker. You
    were sent to your locker by your science teacher be-
    cause you had brought some material he wanted the
    rest of the class to see. At your locker, one of your
    friends stops and asks what you are doing. Right
    then, another teacher comes rushing out of the
    classroom by your locker and says, "What's wrong
    with you? Don't you know any better? Any more

loud noise and you are going to the office!"

2. You are the second son of a middle-class family. Your older brother has always been popular and well-liked. You have always felt you were as good at getting dates as he was. For the past three years, you have wanted to ask out Julie, but you were afraid she would turn you down. Rather than being rejected, you never asked her out. Tonight you have decided you are going to ask her to a movie. You have just dialed her number. Her sister answers the phone and you ask, "May I speak to Julie?" Then Julie comes to the phone and you say, "Julie, this is Bill; I know this is late in the week but I would really like to take you to that movie this weekend. Would you like to go?" After a few seconds pause, Julie begins to laugh very nervously. For some reason, she sounds as if she is feeling awkward.

3. You are the parent. Your ten-year-old son comes home from school and slams the door. You ask, "How was you day, Steve?" Instead of answering you, he tromps into his bedroom and slams that door.

4. You are the teenage daughter. You have been to a party with some friends. Your parents made you promise to be home at 11:00 that night since it was a school night. You walk in the door and see both of your parents waiting in the living room for you. As you walk in the door, your dad says, "It's about time you are home. Where have you been?"

The last example should be used as a way of showing the variability of active listening. That is, there is more than one way to communicate active listening. In this case, active listening might involve, first of all, answering the question, "Where have you been?" Then, the active listening might also include an apology, such as, "I really am sorry if I had you worried." It is active listening because it involves active interpretation of the feelings of the parents. But an additional element is added—the apology for contributing to those feelings.

These examples may be used several ways. It is usually

preferable to have all of the stress reactions, including active listening, shown for each example. You will note that there are examples for teacher problems, parent problems, peer problems and parent-child problems with parenting skills being emphasized.

When You Own the Problem

When you are experiencing some problem involving, perhaps, interpersonal stress, a different set of skills is needed to cope with the difficulty. The languaging skills that have been earlier introduced will now be utilized to cope with this stress. It may be necessary to review some of the languaging skills presented on page 124. The strategy is to present some of the same situations that were dramatized when the other person owned the problem (pages 157-158). This time, however, the other side, or the person who owned the stress, will be re-enacted. Here are some ways situations can be presented for role playing reenactment if you own the problem:

1. You are the teacher. Your class is taking a very important test. Some of your students may or may not receive scholarships to their chosen university depending upon their performance on THIS test. All of a sudden, the silence of test-taking is interrupted by students standing outside your class making noise and disturbing your class.

   A. Each group is to reenact this situation, with the designated 'teacher' handling the problem by (1) blaming, (2) surrendering, (3) ignoring, and (4) using learned languaging skills. The designated 'teacher' might say, *"Looks to me like this noise is bothering some of my students taking their test. I really don't like that because I'm afraid they might not do as well. Would you mind going somewhere else or holding it down?"*

2. Your name is Julie. You have just received a telephone call from Ron, a boy you have always liked, but who has never asked you out. Tonight he is asking you out. You feel a mixture of emotions.

You are embarrassed because your sister is listening. You have just told Jeff that you would "go" with him but you are really happy about Ron asking you out.

    A.   Each group is to reenact this situation similar to the way the first one was reenacted.

3.   Pretend you are a ten-year-old boy named Martin. You have just been cut from the basketball team. You are walking into the house and your mom asks, "How was you day, Martin?"

    A.   Again, the situation should be role played with the various ways showing how Martin could handle the situation.

4.   You are the parents of a teenage daughter. You have asked her to be home at 11:00 that night. Since it was a school night, you didn't really want her to go out in the first place but it was a class event so you compromised and were very firm about the curfew. She walks in the door at 11:30 p.m. You have been worried sick.

    A.   As a parent, use blaming, surrendering, ignoring, as well as languaging skills, to deal with this problem.

Discussion is very important following the dramatizations of these situations. Points for discussions include primarily: (1) What are the consequences for each way of handling these problems? (2) How did you feel with each 'position?' (3) What do you think would have been some feelings of the other person for the different ways of dealing with stress? and (4) Did any of the methods make you feel LESS stressful/more stressful? By the way, these same discussion points could be relevant at the end of situations on pages 157 and 158, when the other person owned the problem.

Parenting and Teaching

The parent-child and teacher-child relationships are crucial to the formation of the child's personality. The child must feel a warmth and caring attitude on the part of these very important adults.

The relationship:

The younger the child, the more he or shee needs to have a close relationship with the parents. Yet, when our children are young—when they need us most—usually happens at a time in the lives of the parental adults when they, the adults, are trying to catch hold of their own life's dreams. As these young parents try on life's uniforms and attempt to form their niche that will be with them for the rest of their lives, precious little time is left for their children.

To start off the initial presentation on parenting, here is a story that could be read to the entire class:

Lee was born in 1939, two months after his father had died. Out of necessity, Lee's mother had to look to other people to help raise Lee. HIs mother married for the third time when he was five-and-one-half years old. And briefly, Lee experienced a close interpersonal attachment with an important person. But not for long. In only one of a long series of disappointments, this relationship was brought to a halt when his mother divorced his stepfather. This happened when Lee was eight years old.

In school, Lee had to fend for himself. He had to get his own meals at noon and after school. He took care of himself in the mornings. Often his mother left him in the car for hours while she worked as a saleslady. At school he had no friends, had difficulty in communicating, and acted withdrawn. Although he was a discipline problem, Lee's mother refused to cooperate with school authorities. At one point, before any positive action could be taken, his mother moved out of state because of the problems he was experiencing at school. By the time Lee was seventeen, he had lived in five different cities and in twenty-three different homes. He had attended twelve different schools while he completed nine grades. But neither Lee nor his mother could escape from their problems and failures.

He stumbled from failure to failure. No one failed at more things than Lee. In apparent desperation, he joined the Marines. This also was no solution. His three years in the marines resulted in two court martials and an undesirable discharge. Still another failure.

161

Lee sought solace in the Soviet Union. When he was told that he could no longer remain there, he attempted suicide. No one wanted him. Everywhere he turned, he was rejected. He had nowhere to go.

He did manage to marry a girl by the name of Marina. But the marriage, like everything else, failed. On the evening of November 21, Lee emotionally took a risk. He went to his wife's apartment house to try to get back together. Instead, he experienced the ultimate rejection. He was hurt by the one person who meant the most to him. No one will ever know what emotions Lee experienced that night. One thing is certain. That painful sense of rejection and isolation exploded. The next day he struck out against the world. On November 22, 1963, Lee Harvey Oswald assassinated President John F. Kennedy.

Perhaps other people were involved. Perhaps not. Probably we will never know for sure. But it should be obvious that Lee's life history was a much more powerful conspirator than anyone else could have been.

Actually, the story of Lee was told only to make you understand that similar tragic stories could have been told about any one of a number of parent-child tragedies. For example, similar stories could have been told about:

*Any one of five children a day who is murdered each and every day BY PARENTS because that child didn't behave the way the parent thought was appropriate.
*Any one of 10,000 children who is severely battered by parents each year.
*Any one of four million incidents of child abuse that occurs in these United States each year.

At this point, the material that is presented on pages 60-66 could be taught to the class. This material is of crucial importance and it is vital that the students be aware of these principles before proceeding. From that material, the point should not be lost that more time should be spent catching the child at being good than is spent catching the child at being bad.

Here is a series of situations that many parents find themselves in. One session could be spent on each of these situations.

162

For each situation, students may be asked to identify blaming responses, surrendering responses, ignoring responses and languaging with appropriate consequences. Then there should be class discussion about the best possible way of handling each situation.

Situation No. 1: You are at the grocery store. Your three-year-old begins crying VERY LOUDLY for a candy bar.

Situation No. 2: Your five-year-old son knocks down a four-year-old girl and takes her tricycle.

Situation No. 3: Your thirteen-month-old baby cries every time you put her in her bed. She wants to sleep with you. (The point should be made here that no complex languaging is necessary but that appropriate consequences are. For instance, the appropriate consequence should be to IGNORE the cries and to keep putting her back in her bed.)

Situation No. 4: Your six-year-old is crying because you won't let him watch his favorite television show. You have a room full of company and there is no room for his TV.

Situation No. 5: Your daughter is one-year-old. Right after her birthday party, she begins walking across the street. (The point should be made here that spanking a child is the appropriate consequence but it must be hard enough to hurt and it MUST HAPPEN RIGHT AS THE CHILD IS TAKING THE FIRST STEPS INTO THE STREET.)

Situation No. 6: As your son and daughter are walking outside to play, your son jabs your daughter in the stomach hard enough to make her cry. (The point should be made here that sometimes consequences must be manufactured, or made up. There isn't always an easy, natural consequence that seems to fit. But there still must be discipline. An example here would be having the son sit on the divan for a period of time. The period of time will be determined by how hard he hit his sister. If the sister were really hurt, a half hour may be necessary. Lesser time would be appropriate for a less severe blow. Languaging skills should also accompany the manufacturing of consequences.)

Situation No. 7: As a teacher, one of your students has just thrown a desk over, spilling and turning over all of the belongings of another student.

Situation No. 8: As a teacher, one of your students is refusing to do any work.

Other situations: Students should be encouraged to bring situations involving parenting and teaching so that these types of alternatives may be discussed.

What would you do if:

Students need practice learning to deal with positive situations as well as stressful ones. Class discussion generated by these examples can be quite helpful in guiding their thinking.

Situation No. 1: Your son has just helped clear the table after dinner without being asked. What would you do?

Situation No. 2: Brian and Vickie, your four-year-old son and six-year-old daughter, have just played together for 35 minutes very cooperatively without any arguments. What would you do?

Situation No. 3: As a teacher you have just caught Tom working five minutes on a math assignment. That is the longest he has ever worked on math. What would you do?

Situation No. 4: Cory, your ten-year-old son, has just behaved beautifully Saturday afternoon. He has helped you mowing the lawn. He even did some trimming around the sidewalk. What would you do?

Situation No. 5: Johnny has a history of being aggressive toward other students. He does a lot of hitting and kicking. But for the past day and a half, he has not kicked or hit anyone. What would you do?

Other Situations: Again, students should be encouraged to think of situations and about how to handle these positive behaviors.

REFERENCES

Gordon, T., *Parent Effectiveness Training*. NY: Peter H. Wyden, Inc., 1971.

Maslow, A., *Motivation and Personality*. NY: Harper, 1954.

Pavlov, I. P., *Conditioned Reflexes*. (Translated by Anrep, G. V.) London: Oxford University Press, 1927.

Plato, from *The Laws*, Book VII, 804 D, Vol. II, p. 57, Harvard University Press, 1930-1935.

Satir, V., Stachowiak, J., and Taschman, H., *Helping Families To Change* (Tiffany, D., Cohen, J., Robinson, A., and Ogburn, K. D., Eds.), Jason Aronson, Inc., 1975.